# LIGHTING
## for a beautiful home

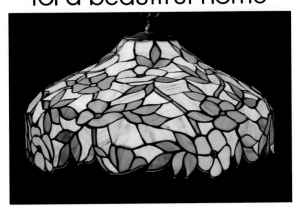

LIGHTING

Published 1988 by Merehurst Limited
Reprinted 1993 by Premier Books
An imprint of Merehurst Limited
Ferry House, 51-57 Lacy Road, Putney,
London SW15 1PR

© Text copyright Jan Orchard 1990
© Copyright Merehurst Limited 1990

Printed in Hong Kong by Leefung–Asco Printers Ltd

ISBN 1 897730 05 5

**Title page** This ultra-modern table lamp of
translucent marble casts interesting
patterns of light on the surrounding walls.

**Half title page** A Tiffany-style, stained
glass pendant lamp with an intricate
pattern of flowers and leaves.

**Contents page** Inspired by Tiffany, this six-
branched table lamp provides a good light
for reading and would look stunning in any
style of room, whether modern or
traditional.

# LIGHTING
## for a beautiful home

Jan Orchard

Jan Orchard

LIGHTING

PREMIER
EDITIONS

# CONTENTS

INTRODUCTION 6

CHAPTER 1
LIVING ROOMS & HALLS 26

CHAPTER 2
KITCHENS & BATHROOMS 52

CHAPTER 3
BEDROOMS 66

CHAPTER 4
GARDENS 78

CHAPTER 5
VISUAL TRICKS 88

CHAPTER 6
UNDERSTANDING LIGHTING 96

CHAPTER 7
SHADES TO MAKE 132

CHAPTER 8
BUYING ANTIQUE FITTINGS 142

MANUFACTURERS & SUPPLIERS 146

**Above** One of the greatest design innovators of the twentieth century, Louis Comfort Tiffany has influenced countless lighting schemes. This Tiffany-style lamp, incorporating a design of cobwebs, closely imitates the master. *Christopher Wray's Lighting Emporium.*

Today we take instant light for granted, yet as little as thirty years ago there were many areas of rural Britain without electricity. I was born and brought up in Cumbria — electricity did not reach us until 1964 and then took a year to get there as cables had to be laid over several miles to reach our remote village. Until then, we had lived with the friendly golden glow and companionable hiss of gas light. Homes outside the village relied on oil lamps; cooking was on a range; laundry done in a giant copper or boiler, called a setpot, with a fire beneath. The radio ran on acid accumulator batteries, which could be re-charged at the local garage.

My great aunt who died in the late 1970s never had electric light — she did not trust any sort of fuel that she could not see or smell, and in that rural backwater, there were many other old ladies like her. Even when power did come, it was unreliable and always failed during thunderstorms — a fact hard to imagine in today's high-tech world.

Primitive man discovered light when he discovered fire — and relied on burning brands for illumination. The Egyptians, Greeks and Romans were more sophisticated, using small oil-fed pottery lamps with a wick for domestic lighting. Even so, they rose and slept with the sun; lighting was only used on special occasions. Roman lamps burnt olive oil, which caused smuts on the walls and ceilings — not the sort of thing the average house-proud Roman matron wanted on her frescoes. The use of oil lamps declined with the fall of the Roman Empire, mainly because it became difficult to get olive oil from the south, and partly because the great monastic houses of northern Europe were beginning to produce candles as a side product of bee-keeping.

It was not really until men moved out of their huts and into the great halls and castles of medieval times that interior lighting really made any great

**Above** Iron wall-sconces and brackets were used to hold thick beeswax candles in the great halls of Tudor and Elizabethan England. The candle was impaled on a spike. *Stuart Interiors.*

developments. Even then, light was only for those who enjoyed powerful positions; the poor rose with the sun and went to bed with the dusk. Light was not considered a necessity for the lives of people who spent the day in unrelenting toil; they were only too happy to go to bed after long hours of farm work. More prosperous tenant farmers and yeomen used rush lights which were usually held in an iron stand. These were made from marsh rushes, dipped in oil, or mutton fat.

The centre of life in the medieval castle revolved around the great hall where the lord of the manor, his soldiers, women, servants and dogs lived and ate. The hall was lit by the central fire, which was also used for roasting, and from brands soaked in oil or pitch. These were held in wall-mounted iron baskets called cressets.

Candles were expensive, so only the wealthier people were able to use them. They were used singly, or in great numbers, impaled on metal spikes called piques. Elaborate candlestands made from iron were considered symbols of status. They usually took the form of a cone made up of three or four rings of candle spikes supported on an ornate stand.

Later, hanging candle beams — straight pieces of wood with four or more candle spikes — were developed; these were the forerunners of the elaborate chandeliers of the seventeenth and eighteenth centuries. As well as being part of everyday life, candles played a vital role in church ritual. February 2nd, Candlemas Day, was one of the great Christian feasts of the medieval year. St Mary's Feast of the Candles celebrated Mary presenting the infant Jesus in the Temple at Jerusalem. There she met Simeon, who prophesied that the child would be 'a light to lighten the Gentiles'. Following this story it became traditional on Candlemas day to bless lights and candles in

**Below** The chandelier developed
from simple hanging beams studded
with spikes to hold candles, and first
appeared in the sixteenth century.
Present-day copies use realistic
candlelight bulbs — much less
messy than the original smoky,
smelly candles. *Stuart Interiors*.

**Below** An early chandelier shows clearly how the design developed from simple wall spikes and sconces. Here, the sort of fittings used on walls have been attached to a simple circle of metal. *Stuart Interiors.*

**Right** Floor-standing pyramids of candles were a status symbol in medieval England — and were usually only seen in great halls and palaces. The ordinary people made do with tallow dips or rush lights. *Stuart Interiors.*

churches. Candlemas Day fell at a time of year when the days were light enough to allow people to work indoors without candles — as a couplet of the time explains: 'Candlemas Day, plant beans in the clay/Put candles and candlesticks all away.'

The practice of holding a candle in a stick, rather than impaling it on a spike, was not realized until the sixteenth century. Elaborate branched designs developed from the first simple candlesticks and were made in wood, wrought iron, silver, gold and brass. Candelabra appeared in seventeenth-century England and were made in silver or in crystal. Crystal was, curiously enough, far more prized than silver — simply because it was more expensive.

One purely practical reason for the development of elaborate candlesticks was that the practice of

**Above** Wall lights like this became popular in the eighteenth century and had the advantage of protecting the walls and ceiling from smoke marks. *Tempus Stet Ltd.*

having servants standing around holding candles quickly proved to be rather dangerous. Charles IV of France is said to have been driven mad by seeing several people burnt to death at a ball when a careless servant set fire to the dancers' clothing.

Candlesticks developed from simple holders to quite ornate affairs, some fitted with ratchets so that the candle could be moved up the stick as it burnt down, keeping the light at the right height for reading.

Candle ends were greatly prized and in many great houses became perks for senior servants. Looking after the candles took an army of servants, not only to keep the candelabra and candlesticks stocked, but also to clean up dripping wax and wipe away smuts. Candles and oil lamps continued as the only form of lighting until town gas became available in the 1780s. The greatest development of the age was the introduction of crystal chandeliers into the homes of the rich, but candles continued to be expensive; in his diary Samuel Pepys complains of the number used in his home. Hundreds would be burnt at a ball or a gala evening in one of the great houses of the period. Even on an ordinary day, a wealthy family could easily use up to a hundred candles.

Cheap tallow candles, the alternative to beeswax, as used by poorer people, were smoky and smelly — life in a well-lit house cannot have been very fragrant!

However in the early nineteenth century candles improved with the discovery of a wax-hardening process. Spermaceti candles, one of the many products to come from the mass slaughter of whales — a thriving industry at that time — gave a better light and lasted longer.

Oil lamps were improved, especially with the increased availability of paraffin. Lamps were made from brass, engraved or coloured glass or from

**Below and right** Oil lamps were beautifully ornate. Engraved or coloured glass, flower-sprigged enamel or china and highly polished brass were favourite materials. Originals can still be found today at reasonable cost. *Temple Lighting.*

**Below** Wall-mounted oil lamps became an important part of interior decor in the Victorian home. Lights were often positioned near a mirror, so that the reflection increased illumination. *Christopher Wray's Lighting Emporium.*

**Left and bottom** Early gas fittings, like the two examples shown here, took much of their design inspiration from oil lamps. The arrival of the incandescent gauze mantle meant that light could be controlled — usually by means of a chain which reduced or increased the gas supply. *Roy Smith & Son.*

flowered china and their light could be controlled by turning the wick up or down. Examples of these old-fashioned lamps can still be found today, and there are many reproduction designs which use electricity instead of oil.

William Murdoch was the first Briton to use gas commercially. He produced gas by distilling coal in a retort, and used it to light his home in Cornwall. Gas was soon introduced into the great mills of the north — extending an already long working day — and was used to light Pall Mall in London.

Gas lighting was not widely used in the home until the invention of the incandescent gauze gas mantle in 1893, which gave a much better, whiter light than the old gas jet.

Gas lighting was first used in wealthier homes, but by the early-1900s had spread to the terraced cottages built by mine and mill owners to house the labour force needed to run the mighty machinery of the industrial revolution. Fittings mostly copied those made for candles or for oil lamps. Hanging gas lamps usually incorporated two or three burners supported on curved brass arms. The incandescent mantles were shaded by plain or coloured glass shades. Wall-mounted fittings followed similar curving lines and were the perfect style to complement the opulence of Edwardian Britain. Gas was also introduced for street lighting, and elaborate lamps became a feature of Edwardian London.

The greatest lighting revolution of all was, of course, the use of electricity. Sir Humphry Davy (1778-1829) was the first man to use electricity for lighting, with his arc lights in 1877. These were, unfortunately, far too bright to be of practical use. Thomas Edison (1847-1931) in America, saw the arc lights, and decided to develop a way of taming electricity to give a softer light that was less harsh and easier to live with.

**Right and below** Curves were almost the hallmark of Edwardian style — and were reflected in light fittings. Shades for gas lamps were either of opaque or patterned glass, usually with a frilly edge, or of painted china, like the bedroom example shown here. *Roy Smith & Son; Temple Lighting.*

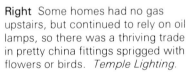

**Right** Some homes had no gas upstairs, but continued to rely on oil lamps, so there was a thriving trade in pretty china fittings sprigged with flowers or birds. *Temple Lighting.*

Edison conducted the first successful trial of the incandescent light bulb on 21 October 1879. At about the same time Sir Joseph Wilson Swan (1828-1914) was working on his version of the incandescent bulb in Britain. In 1880, Edison opened his first light-bulb factory, closely followed by Swan in 1881. A dispute concerning infringement of patents followed, but was resolved when Swan and Edison formed the Edison Swan Electric Light Company in Newcastle.

In 1880, the self-made millionaire Sir William Armstrong had become the first British householder to have a home built with electric light installation. The house was built for him by the architect Norman Shaw and incorporated electric fittings in every room. It was looked upon as an impossibly impractical extravagance; there were even doubts about the safety of electric light, with claims that it affected eyesight and general health. Despite these doubts, during the next 20 years electricity was widely installed in the houses of the wealthy. Consequently, with electricity becoming more freely available and a practical proposition for the home, lighting designers were able to give full rein to ideas formerly impossible to achieve because of the limitations of candles, oil and gas.

The introduction of the light bulb meant that lamps need not now be shaded by fireproof glass or metal and fabric, and so parchment and paper lampshades were introduced. Although a lot of old ideas were simply adapted to electricity, there were new and exciting designs, initially inspired by Art Nouveau and Art Deco design concepts, advancing gradually towards the ultra-modern styling of today. But to begin with, the only truly original designs came from Louis Comfort Tiffany, in New York. These were strongly influenced by Art Nouveau and featured flowers and leaves in stained glass.

**Above** Early electrical fittings were similar in appearance to those designed for use with gas. This Art Nouveau-inspired ceiling fitting is an early example of a design that takes advantage of the freedom offered by a fuel which did not rely on a flame. *R & S Robertson Ltd.*

**Above** Tiffany, the king of lighting design, took much of his inspiration from nature, basing many of his ideas on the shapes of flowers and leaves. Others were quick to copy. This table lamp is the work of a French designer. *Antique Decor, Melbourne, Australia.*

## Art Nouveau

The sweeping, flowing lines of Art Nouveau styling were a reflection of the new freedom from the stiff, corseted years of Queen Victoria. Light fittings, particularly table lamps, featured sculpted female figures, scantily clad and posing gracefully as angels or goddesses and holding aloft globes or flaming torches — lit, of course, by electricity.

Women and flowers were the twin themes of Art Nouveau — and lighting was ideally suited to both of these motifs. Designers let their imagination run riot with elaborate flower-head shades made from opaque coloured glass, supported by a curving brass stem, often entwined with metal leaves. The only drawback to this was that the shade cut out much of the light from the bulb, giving the interiors of the period their typically dim appearance.

There was a passion for 'matching sets', and small bronze founders would commission an artist or sculptor to design a piece, then use it as the basis for light fittings, lamps, ashtrays, vases, epergnes and a host of bric-à-brac.

The greatest influence on lighting design was undoubtedly Louis Comfort Tiffany (1848-1933), an artist in glass whose work is still widely copied. Tiffany trained as a painter, then became an interior designer. Although he lived and worked in New York, he was greatly inspired by England's 'greenery yellery young men' — William Blake (1757-1827), Sir Edward Burne Jones (1833-1898) and Aubrey Beardsley (1872-1898), among others, and by the 1880s passion for the deep, jewel colours of the Orient. His other great love was the representation of natural plant forms in art; leaves, flowers, stems and buds were the prevalent feature of his work.

Tiffany began experimenting with paint on glass, and became one of the principal designers of stained glass windows for churches. There are Tiffany

**Left and below left** Art Deco, with its simple shapes and clean, straight lines was the antithesis of the flowing curves of Art Nouveau. Female figures were a popular and recurring theme. *Libra Designs Art Deco.*

**Below** More Tiffany inspiration, again from France. The flowers are made from cloudy glass, the leaves and figures from metal. Lamps like this are rare and command a high price. *Antique Decor, Melbourne, Australia.*

# INTRODUCTION

**Below and far right** The technique of injecting swirls of colour into glass opened up a world of possibilities for lighting designers. Tiffany was the master of this technique (called favrile) and used it for shades on his flower lamps. These two examples, both French, are good examples of this sort of work. *Antique Decor, Melbourne, Australia.*

**Below** The type of shade everyone recognizes as Tiffany, has coloured glass sections held together by leading or by copper foil. This is a modern-day copy of an original design. *Celtic Glass, Toronto, Canada,*

windows in churches in most of the American states, one or two in England and even examples as far away as Australia. After several years of making coloured glass for natural light to shine through, he began to think about combining coloured glass with artifical light. When Thomas Edison was appointed to the task of electrifying the Lyceum Theatre in New York, Tiffany designed sconces for the footlights. In 1889, he went to the Paris Exposition and saw iridescent glass. Inspired, Tiffany returned to New York to work on lamps using the material.

By 1896, he was selling 'portable Tiffany lamps'. These were oil lamps, which he bought ready-made, adding his own iridescent glass shades and unmistakeable flower and leaf decoration. Demand was so great that he decided to buy his own bronze foundry in order to produce bases which he designed himself.

The first combination of coloured glass and lead — what we today call the Tiffany shade — appeared in 1898. It was an instant success and hundreds more designs, all based on the shapes of flowers and plants, were produced over the next 10 years.

Producing the lamps was labour intensive — colouring and assembly was all by hand, so it is not surprising that by 1905 there were 200 craftsmen working in Tiffany's studio, producing a fantastic garden of glass flowers. There were lamps in the shape of lilies, designed either as single flower forms or in huge, glowing bouquets — bluebells, clematis,

**Left** The Tiffany studio was an electrical garden of lilies, bluebells, clematis, paeonies and other blooms, used singly or assembled to make a bouquet of lights. Original Tiffany flowers are collector's pieces — but good twentieth-century copies like the example shown here, are easy to find. *Christopher Wray's Lighting Emporium.*

**Above** This Tiffany-style lamp in rich glowing colours would be an attractive addition to any period interior. *Christopher Wray's Lighting Emporium.*

cyclamen, paeonies, roses — with the flex fed up to the bulb through a sinuously curving stem of brass or bronze. The famous leaded-glass Tiffany dome-shaped shades bloomed with friezes of stylized flowers in rich, glowing colours.

Tiffany worked in glass for years to achieve the medieval look he really sought to imitate, eventually producing his own version of the style and developing a coloured glass which he termed Favrile glass. The exact method for producing this glass, involving the injection of colour by hand, is extremely complicated. As a result few have copied Tiffany's work successfully and no one has ever been able to produce work of a comparable quality. Tiffany retired from the company in 1919 and, from then on, the quality of both workmanship and design declined. Finally in 1938, five years after he had died, the firm went into liquidation. Original Tiffany lamps are collector's pieces — a good example will sell today for several thousand pounds. Luckily, for those who want to re-create the Tiffany look, there are copies available from high street stores and lighting specialists; these may not be as beautiful as the original examples, but make attractive additions to any period interior.

**Art Deco**

The harsh realities of the First World War put an end to the flowing romanticism of Art Nouveau. Art Deco, the style of the jazz age could not have been more different. Lines were straight rather than curved; shapes were geometric rather than natural. 'Form must follow function' was the designer's creed — and Art Deco was a prime example of this maxim. Colours used in light fittings were strong and harsh — vivid oranges, bright greens, strong purples, a particularly shrieking shade of crimson, often combined with the shine of chromium.

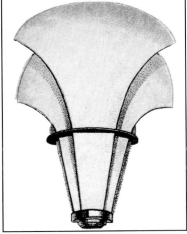

**Left and above**  The jazz age comes to lighting. The glitter of chrome, combined with strong colours and geometric shapes reflected the new realism as the golden Edwardian days were replaced by the harshness of the war to end all wars. *Dernier & Hamlyn Ltd.*

**Right** A French cameo glass table lamp, designed in 1922 by Charles Schneider. *The Lamp Gallery.*

**Below** This striking Art Nouveau lamp is not only functional but decorative and would become a striking feature in any room. *The Lamp Gallery.*

**Below right** Where subtle lighting is desired this painted glass shade would cast a delicate glow. *Temple Lighting.*

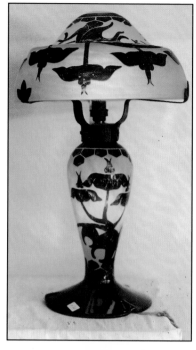

When Tutankhamun's tomb was discovered in 1922, the Egyptian look became a major influence — reflected in pyramid-shaped wall lights and table lamps that enjoyed a popular fashion. The craftsmanship of Tiffany's day was gone — Deco fittings were mass-produced using cheap, factory-made materials. Consequently, they did not last, so it is rather difficult to find original Art Deco lamps today. However good copies are always available from lighting specialists.

**To the Modern Day**

Fluorescent light was introduced at the New York World's Fair in 1939, and immediately became popular as a working light. Early fluorescents gave a harsh, white unflattering light, though present-day versions are colour corrected and give a kinder light.

Major developments took place in commercial building schemes. As early as 1930, the architect Le Corbusier (1887-1965) was looking at ways to incorporate lighting systems into buildings with the object of increasing the sense of space in an interior.

Wars have a habit of changing styles — and the Second World War was no exception. Out went the colour of Deco, in came the almost Scandinavian simplicity of the style that became known as 'contemporary'. Table lamps and light fittings were made from teak, or from black wrought iron. Shades were simple plastic cones or of pleated paper. Fluorescent lights came out of offices and into kitchens — although the light was harsh and unflattering.

It was not until the home revolution of the 1960s, when Terence Conran encouraged young, forward-thinking Britons to think of their homes as a well-designed space for living, rather than somewhere to put the furniture, that home lighting began to move away from the conventional arrangement of a single pendant light backed with a couple of table lamps. The early branches of Habitat sold spotlights — suddenly light became directional. Development has been non-stop since then. Downlighters and dimmers, once only used in commercial schemes, are now freely available for domestic use. Fittings such as these all filtered through to domestic use from the commercial world. In the last 10 to 15 years changes have been particularly dramatic. The most important new development is probably the low-voltage bulb which works on 6, 12 or 24 volts (rather than the usual 240), is economical to run and gives a clear, white light.

There is a greater choice of fittings and equipment to create special effects than ever before — whatever the style or age of your home. Specialist lighting shops provide styles to suit every interior, every taste and every budget. Lighting your home, both beautifully and effectively, has never been simpler and I hope that in this book you will see the many possibilities offered by good, well-planned lighting for making your home a more comfortable and attractive place in which to live.

## CHAPTER 1

**Right** Table lamps are a living room essential. Use them to create pools of light in dark corners and near seating areas. Choose fittings for their decorative values, as well as for their pratical use. *John Cullen Lighting.*

**Above** Wall lamps help to break up long, straight expanses, and create interesting pools of light. Choose lamps to suit the style of your room. Good period copies, like this, are easy to find. *The End of Day Lighting Company.*

The family living room can truly be described as a room for all reasons. A combination of rest room, entertainment centre, study, playroom, music room, library and what used, in a more gracious age, to be called a receiving room, it is a complex area to plan, to decorate and to light.

The best way to approach the problem is to imagine an average day and then make a list of the ways in which the living room is used. This will give a starting point for the lighting scheme, whether it be a matter of making the best of existing facilities, or of starting afresh.

**Improving an Existing Scheme**

Sometimes the restrictions of a tight budget, or the fact that the house is rented or will be yours for only a short time, makes re-planning lighting impossible and impractical.

The living room lighting scheme likely to be found in an 'unimproved' home usually consists of a central pendant light, one or two table lamps and a couple of wall lights. In this sort of situation, the central pendant is rarely used because it casts a bright, uniformly unflattering light over the room. Most people favour a combination of wall lights and table lamps for illumination. These create a better atmosphere than the central light alone, but are not particularly adaptable.

How can this sort of scheme be changed without carrying out expensive re-wiring? The answer is simple. Begin by introducing some flexibility, by replacing conventional light switches for the central pendant and the wall lights with dimmer switches. You can then enjoy gentle background light from the pendant and spots of warmer accent from the wall lights by dimming pendant and wall lights to different levels.

Look carefully, too, at the fittings. A pendant

**This page and opposite** Keeping light fittings in sympathy with the style of the room is an essential. All of these designs would live happily with 30s Deco styling, or with simple modern furniture.

light with one bulb and a small shade will produce a bright, rather uncomfortable light. Consider replacing it with a branched pendant, or look for a wider, flatter shade, so that light is spread outwards. Giant ball-shaped oriental paper shades are cheap, look effective and soften the light from a central pendant.

A chandelier, either of glass or brass is a good choice in a period setting. Before you have a chandelier installed, make sure that both the ceiling and the chain from which it is suspended are strong enough to hold the fitting. Chandeliers take small, candle-shaped bulbs available in 25, 40 and 60 watt sizes. These can be plain or can have a flickering effect — supposed to imitate candlelight, but usually irritating rather than effective. Low-wattage bulbs provide the softest effect — a chandelier fitted with high-wattage candle bulbs can be unpleasantly dazzling.

Make the most of a high ceiling by fitting the central pendant with a shade wider at the top than at the bottom so that light is beamed upwards.

You could even replace the central pendant with a rise-and-fall fitting on an extra long cable pulled low over a coffee table to light a display of plants or a collection. Use a crown silvered bulb to direct all the light downwards and to prevent it from dazzling anyone sitting around the table.

Chain store wall lights of the 1960s and 70s can be an unwelcome inheritance for home owners. In a Victorian or Edwardian terraced house they do not fit in easily with traditional features like fireplaces, cornices and ceiling roses. Although it is true to say that some of the really spectacular modern and period fittings on the market are extremely expensive, it is possible to find low-priced versions of the most popular styles in high street stores and DIY superstores.

**Opposite page:** *Davniglass Handcraft; R & S Robertson Ltd.* **This page:** *Libra Designs Art Deco; R & S Robertson Ltd.*

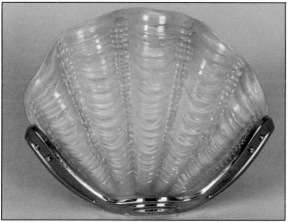

When replacing wall lights think carefully about the style of the room. If you are a new home owner and have not yet bought the bulk of the furniture or settled on an overall decorative scheme, simple half shells in opaque glass or in plaster are a good choice as they will harmonize with most styles. These lights beam up to the ceiling, washing the wall in a soft, warm glow.

Extending-arm lights in brass, with fabric shades, are another good, all-purpose choice, doubling as task lighting when a chair is positioned so that the light, when extended, gives just the right sort of illumination for reading.

Period sconces (decorative fittings, often in the shape of a flambeau, a swag or a rope) either with bare candle bulbs or with tiny shades, are increasingly popular but are expensive. Think

**Below** If you have a large, impressive picture, worth showing off, draw attention to it with well designed lighting. Here, the picture is lit from above by directional downlights, and accented by wall-mounted fittings. *John Cullen Lighting.*

carefully before you buy one of these as you will probably have to live with this purchase for some time. Avoid brightly gilded sconces; those in dark wood or with faded gilding look far better. The type with bulbs at two different levels look most effective.

Even the drabbest living room can be cheered up with table and standard lamps. These do not have to cost a fortune. Wooden 1950s-style standards can be found at knockdown prices in junkshops and at auctions. If you stain, strip or re-paint the wood and then add a new shade you can give a plain, old standard lamp an instant new lease of life. Choose a shade to pick up another colour in the room, either from the carpets, paintwork or from the upholstery. If the lamp is to stand in a particularly dark corner, choose a light shade as it will cast a better light than a sombre, traditional fabric. The lining of the shade has an effect too; a gold lining gives a soft light, while silver reflects the light outwards. For maximum lighting effect it is best to choose a wide bottomed shade.

Standard lamps, where the beam shines down, make excellent reading lights. You should experiment with the light in various positions so that it casts shadow-free illumination over your book or newspaper. The best location is usually behind the chair and slightly to one side.

Modern uplighter standards can be found at reasonable prices. Their stark, clean lines look best in a room furnished with a few well-chosen pieces of modern furniture, while the beam will make the most of a handsome ceiling. Two or three uplighters fitted with 200 or 300 watt tungsten-halogen bulbs (depending on the size of the room), are a good substitute for ceiling-mounted general lighting.

Table lamps are probably your greatest ally when it comes to cheering up a drab, depressing living room. They come in all shapes and sizes, from small

**Below left** Chandeliers do not just come in crystal. If your interior is Victorian or Edwardian in style, look for an authentic design like this, which combines brass with *pâte de verre* shades.
*R.J. Chelsom & Co Ltd.*

**Left** Wall sconces based on a Regency design are the perfect complement to this classic fireplace.
*Cohen & Pierce Interiors.*

**Above and right** The advent of low-voltage halogen downlighting has revolutionized the way domestic interiors are lit. Low-voltage lighting is ideal for living areas as the fittings can be either fixed or directional. Directional fittings are perfect for highlighting pictures or architectural features. *John Cullen Lighting.*

overheats). A lamp can be wired in with the plug for the television set without causing an electrical overload. Position the lamp to the side and slightly behind and above the set for the right light for viewing. If you then add two or three other lamps in corners of the room, or on a chest or bookshelf half way along a wall, you will succeed in transforming a depressing scene into an instantly warm and welcoming living room.

### Starting Afresh

Few people are lucky enough to move into a property ready-equipped with a well-planned lighting scheme. Even if you leave other lighting improvements until later, the living room is well worth tackling at an early stage.

Because of the many roles of the average family living room, a combination of general, accent and task lighting is needed. The scheme must be carefully planned in advance, taking into account the position of furniture, the height of the ceiling, work areas and

ceramic globes fitted with coolie shades to large Chinese or Indian-inspired pieces, and at all price levels and in all colours.

In an existing wiring layout, you will probably have to position the lamps around the walls, close to sockets (avoid trailing flexes as they are dangerous, and remember never to run a flex under a rug as it can cause a fire if there is a wiring fault and the cable

**Below and far right** Matching fittings give a co-ordinated look which works well in a formal room. This chandelier and matching wall lights are fitted with candle bulbs which flicker to give an authentic candlelight look.
*R & S Robertson Ltd.*

**Left** The collection on the table is highlighted by the table lamp while a directional downlighter angled onto the painting brings it to life.
*John Cullen Lighting.*

the lighting of pictures or a collection.

A good way to begin planning your scheme is to draw up the shape of your living room on squared paper, remembering to indicate doorways and windows, recesses, the fireplace and any other architectural features. You can then mark your preferred positions for major pieces of furniture and pictures. Carefully attach a sheet of tracing paper to the squared paper. If you then mark the positions of lighting, the plan will allow you to see fittings in relation to furniture and architectural features.

### General Lighting

Recessed downlighters undoubtedly provide the best and most effective general lighting for the living room. A mixture of fixed and directional lights allows you to use some of the fittings to highlight architectural features or pictures. Correct spacing of halogen lights is important if the area is to be lit effectively. Your electrician will advise on this. A good electrician should take the planned furniture and features layout into account when planning the position of lights.

**This page** Table lamps add a strongly decorative element to living room lighting, so take time when choosing. Look for interesting designs which can be mixed with simpler fittings. *Davniglass Handcraft; Casa Fina.*

Dimmers are the best way to control general lighting. Have them fitted so that lights can be controlled in blocks — enabling the lights in one area of the room, used perhaps for watching television, to be dim, while others in an area used for reading or study can be bright. This sort of system costs more to install than a single dimmer, but the extra flexibility is well worth the expense.

### Adding for Effect

Once a scheme for general lighting has been decided, think about adding task or accent lighting.

Table lamps are the easiest and most attractive way to add accent lighting. Positioned at the end of a sofa or beside a chair on a low table, on sideboards, shelves and occasional tables, they create pools of warm light — and come in styles to suit almost any sort of decor.

Table lamps need sockets — and this is where careful planning comes in. It is no use discovering that there are not enough outlets, or that they are in entirely the wrong places once rewiring is complete. Mark on your plan where you want to use table lamps. As a guide, they look good in corners, on a low table in the centre of the room, or behind tall plants so that the light shines through the leaves, making an attractive pattern on the ceiling. If you want to use plug-in uplighters, mark these on the same plan as the table lamps, as sockets will be needed.

Lamps intended to be positioned away from the walls should be plugged into floor sockets. A floor socket is an outlet sunk into the floor, covered with a flap when not in use. Installing floor sockets is far better, and safer, than trailing cable across carpeting.

It is worth shopping around to find exactly the right lamps. It is a mistake to think that they must all

**Below** Classic crystal chandeliers vary from the fairly simple, as shown here, to designs more at home in the Palace of Versailles than in a domestic interior. Chandeliers need a high ceiling to be really effective. *John Cullen Lighting.*

**Right** Use a table lamp and a
couple of comfortable chairs to
create a quiet corner in the living
room. *Cohen & Pearce Period
Interiors.*

**Right** If you are lucky enough to
have a beautiful ceiling like this, use
uplighters to show it to advantage.
Chandeliers and wall sconces are
ideal in a period setting.
*Cohen & Pearce Period Interiors.*

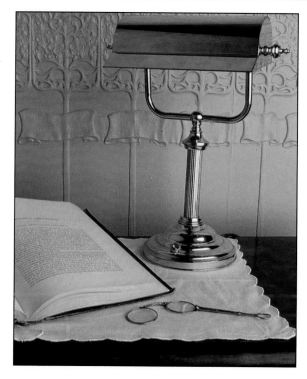

be of the same style and in the same colour. As a general guide, the only place where a matching pair of lamps is desirable is at each end of a sideboard or console table. For the biggest lamps, choose a colour either to complement or contrast with the predominant shade of the colour scheme. If, for instance, the main colour in the room is blue, two large blue and white Chinese lamps with cream shades would look good. If there is a strong pattern on upholstery or curtains, look for plain lamp bases in a lighter or darker tone.

Where the living room doubles as a study or hobby area, table lamps can be used as task lighting. Lights specially designed for this purpose are better left to the office — unless the style of the room is starkly modern. Traditional brass desk fittings with a long, half-cylindrical shade designed to beam light down on work combine practicality with good looks.

A large room with a high ceiling will benefit from judicious use of wall washers and either wall or floor-mounted uplighters. Wall-mounted uplighters are a useful way to break up a large expanse of wall

**Above and top** Snooker-style
fittings, which can be either rise-
and-fall or fixed, are the perfect way
to light a long, narrow dining table.
Use crown-silvered bulbs so that
diners will not be dazzled.
*The End of Day Lighting Company;*
*R.J. Chelsom & Co Ltd.*

and highlight an interesting cornice. Tall floor-
mounted uplighters are mainly minimalist in style. In
a traditional interior, small drum uplighters which
can be concealed behind a piece of furniture or a
large plant are more appropriate. You can position
the plants and lamp so that the light shines through
the leaves, throwing an interesting pattern onto the
back wall and ceiling.

## Entertaining

Light is an integral part of entertaining, a way to
add atmosphere to every occasion — from a casual
outdoor barbecue to the formality of a full scale
dinner party.

## Dinner Parties

Formal dining is not as fashionable as it used to
be, but even in today's busy families, there are times
when everyone gathers around the table, rather than
relying on meals taken on the run or in front of the
television.

To make dining really intimate and relaxing, the
table should be isolated in an island of light — an
effect which can be achieved in various different
ways.

Tungsten-halogen downlighters positioned above
the dining table, and controlled so that they can be
used bright while the rest of the room is either dark
or dim, turn the dining table into a focal point. In
addition, they provide background for candles.

Rise-and-fall pendants are the time-honoured
fitting for dining, and can be used alone, or in
conjunction with tungsten-halogen dimmers or
candles. If you use a pendant, put candles around the
perimeter of the table, on a sideboard or console,
rather than in the centre.

Badly designed pendants can have the effect of
cutting people off from one another, or of dazzling

**Below** Halogen downlighters, carefully positioned above the dining table and controlled individually, mean that the table can become an island of light. This room is long and narrow — note how positioning the wall of smoked mirror glass behind the table gives the optical illusion of a wider area. *John Cullen Lighting.*

# LIGHT FOR LIVING

them. Avoid this by choosing a design where the bulb fits well up inside the fitting, and use a crown-silvered bulb so that light is reflected back from the fitting onto the table below.

## Christmas

Christmas can truly be described as the feast of lights — a time for candles, the sparkle of baubles and all the magic of tradition.

There are many different types of Christmas tree lights on the market. With a little thought you can put together a striking and unusual arrangement. Perhaps the nicest are mini lights in one colour — of these, white is best. Use them on your Christmas tree, threaded carefully around the branches so that every area of the tree is lit. For a really good effect, you will probably need more than one set of lights — it is perfectly safe to wire up to three sets onto a 13 amp plug. Combine the lights with glittering silver or white ornaments, or for a traditional touch, tie plain red or plaid bows of ribbon to each branch.

Crystal icicles, available from good department stores, will catch the light beautifully, as will mirrored tree decorations and anything with silvery sparkle. In a large room, you can afford the space to have a tall tree. Choose a blue spruce — the foliage is lusher than the traditional Norwegian pine and allows tree lights to be concealed among the needles. Light it from below with a drum uplighter to cast dramatic shadows onto the ceiling and walls.

Christmas lights need not be confined to the tree. Coil them inside clear Perspex boxes for an eye-catching display (perfectly safe as long as you do not go out leaving the lights switched on). Twist them with ribbons into swags of greenery for use on the staircase or above the mantelpiece.

Candles are as traditional at Christmas as mince pies and mulled wine. The Victorians used them on

**Left and below** Ceiling pendants come in all shapes, colours and sizes from simple, single, glass shades to ornate, Victorian reproductions. *R & S Robertson Ltd; Antique Decor, Melbourne, Australia.*

**Below** Blue lenses have been used on the ceiling-mounted spotlights in this room to give a cool, almost underwater feel. *John Cullen Lighting.*

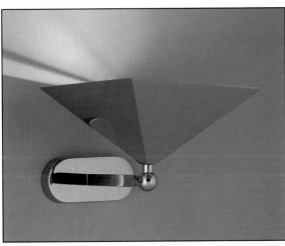

Below and bottom Ultra-modern
uplighters add a touch of the space
age to a minimalist interior. The light
is bounced off the ceiling, giving
uncluttered interiors an atmosphere
of endless light and space.
*R & S Robertson Ltd.*

Christmas trees where they look beautiful but are messy and dangerous. It is still possible to buy both candle holders and candles for use on trees, but they should only be lit when there is no danger of anyone bumping into the tree and setting fire either to themselves or the branches. It is far better to stick to today's safe electrical alternatives.

There are, however, hundreds of other ways in which candles can be used to add to the beauty of your home at Christmas. Look out for Scandinavian crystal Christmas lights. These are in opaque or stained and leaded glass, and are made in the shape of houses, angels, Santa Claus or other symbols of Christmas. A tiny night light stands behind the glass, shining through and flooding the piece with light. They look delightful on a windowsill, or on a low table in a shadowy corner, and are safe enough to use where there are children.

Candles of varying sizes and thicknesses, arranged in a shallow bowl filled with baubles make a decoration everyone loves, especially if you make the most of the display by standing it in front of a mirror. Alternatively, group candlesticks of various heights together to create a flickering pool of light.

Making Christmas candle centrepieces for the table can make for a pretty variation on conventional candles in sticks. Buy a ring-shaped piece of the proprietory foam base used for arranging flowers. Push four tall candles into it and then cover the base with holly, ivy, berries and gilded pine cones and nuts.

Eating by candlelight is romantic at any time of the year, but is especially nice at Christmas. Use candlesticks, or make a Christmas centrepiece as described. Be careful to position the candles towards the centre of the table, so that there is no danger of anyone catching their sleeves on the flame, or knocking the candlestick over. You will find an

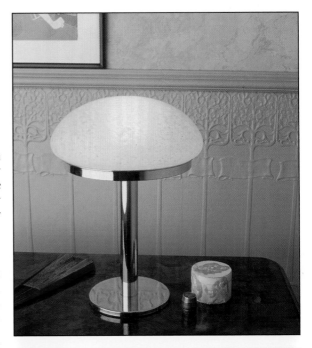

**Right and below** A table lamp in a hall is essential, providing a comfortable glow when the main lights are out, and vital illumination for writing down telephone messages. *The End of Day Lighting Company; R.J. Chelsom & Co Ltd.*

enormous choice of candlesticks for dining, from traditional branched candelabra to simple glass or pottery holders. Plain holders can be given a festive touch at Christmas by winding ivy and thin red or gold ribbon around the stem of the candlestick, or by decorating with bows of red or gold ribbon.

## Halls and Staircases

How many halls have you seen, lit only by a dim overhead pendant, where it is quite possible to risk life and limb falling over bicycles, discarded toys, wellington boots and other household flotsam hidden in the gloom?

It is a great mistake to treat the hall as nothing more than a cross between a dumping ground and a corridor between rooms. The hall gives visitors their first impression of the way you live; it acts as a buffer state between you and the sort of callers you do not want to ask in; in many homes it does duty as a place for the telephone, coats, umbrellas and for displaying collections.

How you light the hall depends initially on its shape and size, on the general decorative scheme and on how the area is used. Whatever the arrangement, a mixture of lighting will always work better than a single source.

## Large Halls

Large, lofty halls in older houses usually have interesting cornices, doorways or ceilings. These are not always worth showing off, but if you have a ceiling or cornice to be proud of, it can be lit by uplighters or wall washers.

Wall-mounted decorative uplighters are best for hall use as floor-standing lights can cause an obstruction. Keep the period and style of the hall in mind when choosing fittings. Simple plaster half circles suit any style, as they can be painted to match

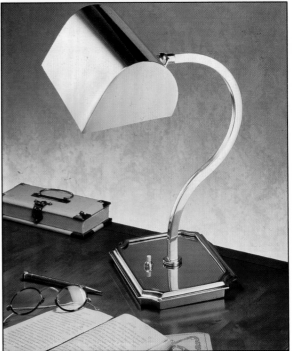

**Below and right** Staircase lighting is a must for safety reasons. A long, curved flight can be lit from above by a chandelier. Straight flights can be lit by downlighters, and by positioning wall lights, like this simple sconce, on half landings. For continuity, use the same design in the hallway. *Mark Wilkinson Furniture Ltd; R & S Robertson Ltd.*

**Above and right** Large halls and staircases lend themselves to elaborate fittings, like the French table lamp and Victorian iron staircase lamp shown here. *Antique Decor, Melbourne, Australia; Ripponlea, Melbourne, Australia, a property of the National Trust.*

the general colour scheme.

A large, period hall lends itself to lighting on a grand scale. It is one of the few areas of the house where you can use a large, decorative pendant, either in combination with complementary wall fittings (traditional brass picture lights can double), table lamps or low-voltage eyeball spots used as accents.

Splendid, many-armed brass pendants can often be found at auctions, and look quite stunning when combined with the warm glow of antique wood furniture, dark panelling, traditional table lamps, chintz and all the other essential ingredients of the country house style. If you buy a light fitting from an antique shop or an auction, always have it checked and installed by a professional electrician.

In a large hall, you may have room for furniture. A chest or console table are traditional choices, and

are the perfect location for a table lamp or two, to add accent. A long, narrow console with a plant, flower display or a large bowl or other piece of china, flanked by two tall table lamps, is a time-honoured scheme which always works well. Another nice idea is to position a modest-sized lamp on a small round table, then arrange a small collection so that the light shines down on it.

If the hall has an alcove, there will probably be room in it for a comfortable chair and a small table or chest. A well thought-out lighting scheme can turn this corner into a cosy retreat for reading or thinking, or a comfortable spot to hold telephone conversations.

General light for the alcove can be provided by a low-voltage directional ceiling fitting. Explain to the electrician what size the alcove is, and what level of light you want to achieve, and he will help you to select the right size bulb. Accent lighting together with a table lamp can be used. As well as creating a warm pool, this will give enough illumination for telephone users to look up numbers and write down messages. Where there is enough wall space for a picture or wall hanging, you can illuminate it with directional wall washers.

If the alcove is simply a small recess and will not house a chair or table, a large flourishing green plant can prove an attractive alternative feature. Position a small floor-standing, drum-shaped uplighter so that the beam shines up through the leaves of the plant, giving an interesting shadow pattern on the walls and ceiling of the recess. It is a good idea to use a grow bulb (available from good electrical shops and from garden centres) if the recess is particularly shady, to encourage the plant to produce leaves and stay green.

Lighting for a large modern hall should be simple with unobtrusive fittings. A mixture of directional ceiling-mounted, low-voltage fittings and recessed

**This page and opposite** If your hall is large, or is an awkward shape, use lighting to create a focal point. This can be achieved by designing a comfortable corner, with a table, chair and plants, or by positioning a light in front of a simple display of pictures. *The Lamp Gallery; Adrian Sankey.*

downlighters is ideal. The directional lights can be used to highlight pictures, while the non-directional downlighters can beam straight down. This is a good way to display a beautiful rug which does not necessarily have to be modern: traditional oriental designs work surprisingly well in contemporary interiors.

It is quite unusual to find an alcove or recess in a modern hallway, but if there is one, treat it in the same way as described for a traditional hall, using simple, well-designed furniture and lighting, to keep lines clean and unfussy.

### Long, Narrow Halls

A long, narrow dark hallway presents a real lighting challenge. Lack of space means that there is very little scope for adding interest with furniture — some narrow shelves or a slim console table are often the most that can be accommodated. A good lighting scheme can make even the gloomiest strip attractive — but careful thought is needed.

The very worst thing to do is to light the area with a single pendant fitting (a mistake many home owners make in the belief that a single light source is all that is needed in a confined space). This sort of fitting will only illuminate the central portion of the corridor, accentuating the general gloom. The way to light a corridor successfully is to use a combination of multiple fittings. At the very simplest level, you can fit a ceiling-mounted track fitted with wide-beam spotlights angled to illuminate the walls. Tilt the lights so that the beam falls on pictures, hangings or a wall-mounted collection, such as plates grouped in fours or sixes, box shelves containing small pieces of china, a display of keys, matchboxes, or whatever your particular passion happens to be.

Accent can be added with a small lamp placed on a narrow console table or a shelf.

Mirrors, either wall-mounted or as part of a hall stand, are favourite pieces of hall furniture. A mirror allows you to check your appearance as you leave the house — and visitors glance at them as they

arrive. Never position lights so that they shine directly into the mirror as anyone standing in front of it will obscure the light source. Wall or table lights flanking the mirror are better, as they light the glass and provide the user with a good, clear view.

## Small Halls

If cottages and terraced houses have a hall at all, it is usually very small, often with standing room only for one or two people. Here the lighting scheme can be a simple combination of a wall washer and an accent light. The wall washer is an ideal way of illuminating a painting or hanging.

The accent can come from wall lights — one on each side — or from a table lamp on a small piece of furniture, if there is room in a corner.

## Security

Hallways should always be fitted with a two-way switch, so that you can turn on the light as soon as you enter the area and again when you leave it. Position one switch close to the front door to avoid having to grope your way through the darkness when you come into the house.

If you are out all day, run the hall lights on a timer so that they switch on as soon as darkness falls. This deters intruders and gives you a warm welcome home. It is also a good idea to fit a switch for outdoor lights by the front door. See the chapter on Gardens and Outdoor Lighting, for more details.

## Staircases

As the staircase leads from the hall, the lighting scheme used must match what is happening below — with some practical additions. For safety's sake stairs must be well lit, especially on half landings or where there is a bend.

On a single, straight staircase, one light source positioned at the top is usually enough when used in combination with other lighting. Directional lighting is best as the beam can be angled to shine downwards — but be careful to position the fitting so that the beam does not dazzle people climbing the stairs.

Accent can be added with pictures lit by traditional picture lights.

Staircases with half landings need a different treatment. Wide-beam downlighters, recessed into the ceiling on each landing, are ideal as the light covers the landing floor area and spills down the stairs.

Staircase lighting should always be controlled by two-way switching. Small children often like to have the stairs lights left on at night. You can also fit dimmers, so that light can be kept at a low but comforting level.

## CHAPTER 2

**Above** Under-unit lighting, where the fittings are concealed by a cornice rail, creates a comfortable glow in this traditional kitchen. *Mark Wilkinson Furniture Ltd.*

**Right** Modern glass wall units, lit from the inside by concealed low-voltage fittings, are an effective way to display china and glass.

The kitchen really is the heart of the home, a place not just for cooking, but for eating, for family get-togethers, homework, play and hobbies. Kitchen styles today range from the traditional farmhouse to the cool, ultra-modern, ultra-efficient European design. But, whatever the look, basic lighting needs remain the same.

### General Lighting

General lighting in the kitchen needs to be strong and clear, so that you can see to work. The worst possible fitting is the central pendant light as anyone standing at a worktop will inevitably be working in shadow. That old favourite, the single fluorescent strip, is better, especially if the kitchen is galley-shaped. But strip lights are not very attractive and soon become traps for airborne grease. There are, however, various other ways to utilize the clear, white light of fluorescent strips, and these will be discussed. The other two choices for general lighting are spotlights on a strip and recessed downlighters. What you choose will depend on your budget and on the size of the room.

### Spotlights

Spotlights on a track are cheap and easy to install (a skilled DIY enthusiast can manage this job with ease). A track or circular ceiling mount fitted with directional spotlights is the ideal choice for a small or galley-shaped kitchen. Use a circular fitting if the kitchen is square; a strip if it is narrow.

Spotlights for the track should be of the wide-beam type. Directed as required, these will light a reasonable area of worktop and cupboard space without casting shadows.

Before installing the track, make sure that wall cupboard doors can still be opened when it is in place. In a very narrow kitchen, where rows of wall

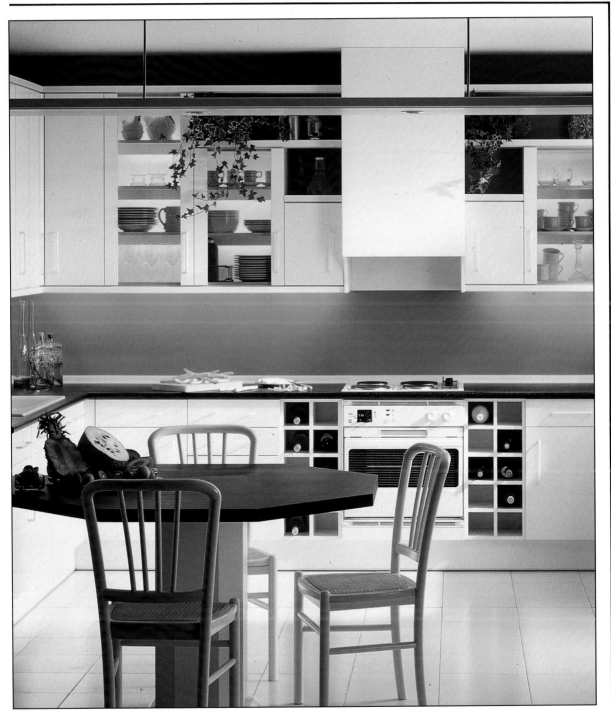

**Below** Strong under-unit lighting
can be used to illuminate working
areas, while halogen downlighters,
controlled by dimmers, provide
general background light.
*John Cullen Lighting.*

cupboards face each other, a track can be totally unsuitable, and you will have to install recessed downlighters instead. To check on whether there is enough clearance space for doors, mark the position of the track on the ceiling. Open your wall unit doors fully. If the edge of the door comes over the pencilled line, a track will not work.

If you do have space to fit a track, when you have installed it, experiment with the spotlights until they beam light to exactly the areas where it is most needed. Target your work areas as the most important. Another good idea is to beam the light to illuminate the insides of large cupboards, so that you can see right to the back.

Galley kitchens that are more than 2m (6½ ft) wide will need two parallel tracks, equally spaced on the ceiling. The light from a single track will not be quite strong enough to penetrate to the corners of a kitchen of this size and will cause shadows. Beware, too, of low ceilings — a track of high-wattage spotlights can cause scalp burns if the ceiling is under 2¼ m (7 ft). It is therefore advisable to choose low-voltage spotlights for this location.

**Fluorescents**

As a source of good, clear working light, fluorescent tubes are hard to beat. Modern tubes are available in daylight tones — avoiding the terrible colour-draining quality often associated with fluorescents. The major drawback is style — a fluorescent tube mounted in the middle of the ceiling will certainly provide an effective means of lighting a small to medium kitchen, but looks unattractive and is inclined to trap airborne grease. One way in which you can take advantage of the lighting quality, without displaying their fittings, is to mount fluorescent tubes on top of wall cupboards (you must allow a space of at least 7½ cm (3 in) between

**Below** Skilled kitchen designers will include lighting when the kitchen is planned, so that important or interesting areas are highlighted. *Cohen & Pearce Period Interiors.*

the top of the cupboard and the ceiling) so that light shines up onto the ceiling. This can look very effective in combination with shiny, high-gloss polyester units. Most kitchen unit ranges have a cornice rail running along the top of wall cupboards; these will effectively conceal the tubes.

**Recessed Downlighters**

Although recessed downlighters are more expensive than either spotlights or fluorescents, the investment is often a worthwhile one. Downlighters suit any style of kitchen, from the ultra-modern Germanic to the comfortable country style. The fittings will not interfere with opening doors and cupboards, and semi-recessed directional lights can be combined with fully recessed static lights when needed. Because the fittings are sunk into the ceiling, they do not collect grease and dust — eliminating a major kitchen cleaning problem.

**This page and opposite** Spotlights on a track are the easiest way to light a galley-shaped kitchen — but make sure that wall-unit doors can be opened fully. A larger, uncompromisingly modern style is best suited to discreet recessed downlights. Many kitchen manufacturers now incorporate lights when the kitchen is built — the modern bird's eye maple and chrome kitchen shown right is a classic example.

## Lighting Extras

Most kitchens built today — be they modern or traditional in style — incorporate strip lighting beneath wall units. This concealed light source is usually switched on with the ceiling lights, and provides good illumination at worktop level. The fittings are concealed by a cornice rail along the bottom of the cupboards. These lights can also be installed into an older kitchen, but you will need to add a decorative cornice strip to the bottom of the cupboards to conceal the bulbs. The lights are inexpensive, cost little to fit, but pay dividends in terms of offering a better working environment.

A good extractor fan is a kitchen essential — there can be few smells less appealing than yesterday's dinner — and reduces airborne grease, helping to keep light fittings clean. All over-hob extractors include a light which comes on when the fans start. This is not merely a gimmick, or a way to add to the price of the machine, but is a useful tool for the cook, shining down into pots and pans, making it easy to see just what is going on. If all you have is a window fan, consider replacing it with an over-hob extractor, not just as an effective method of air-changing, but also as a useful light source. In a traditional kitchen, the extractor and light can be built into a tiled or brick chimney, or into a copper canopy. This means that there is no risk of modern machinery clashing with a rustic atmosphere.

For a warm wood or country-style kitchen, choose downlighters fitted with gold reflectors to give a gentle, golden light. The clear, white light of tungsten-halogen with silver reflectors is a perfect match for laminate, polyester and lacquer finishes.

The latest trend in high quality kitchens, particularly those from Germany, is to build low-voltage eyeball fittings into shelves. These shelves are designed to provide a link between units, or to go

**This page and opposite** Where the kitchen includes a dining area, make sure that there is sufficient light around the table. This can either come from rise-and-fall ceiling fittings or from under-unit lighting combined with ceiling fittings.

This page *Allmilmö*
Opposite *The End of Day Lighting
Company; Mark Wilkinson Furniture  Ltd.*

above a breakfast bar or dining area. A good kitchen specialist will be able to plan a complete lighting scheme for the kitchen to include both the fittings supplied by the manufacturer and ceiling lights of your own choice. Although this kind of personal service is expensive, it is worthwhile since built-in lights and general fittings need to be integrated carefully to give the best overall effect.

## The Kitchen Diner

Very few families make full use of a separate formal dining room, preferring instead to eat in the kitchen on all but special occasions. In a small kitchen, lack of space limits the dining area to a simple worktop and a couple of stools, but in a bigger kitchen, the dining area can be on a grander scale and needs its own distinctive lighting treatment, so that the table can be lit while the rest of the room is in darkness.

The time-honoured solution is a rise-and-fall pendant positioned above the table. These fittings come in a variety of styles and there are many good, traditional designs suitable for farmhouse-style kitchens. One imaginative way to light a long table is to position a row of evenly spaced pendant lights above it. Position them carefully, so that the shades do not separate diners at one side of the table from those at the other — and so that dishes can be put onto the table without the risk of becoming entangled. Fit crown-silvered bulbs, so that light is directed downwards onto the table and does not dazzle those sitting around it.

A rise-and-fall light does not work so well in the clean, uncluttered lines of a modern kitchen, unless you are prepared to hunt for a distinctive, well-designed fitting — and to pay a high price for it. The alternative is to install individually-controlled downlighters or spotlights above the table.

**Below** Bathroom mirrors should be lit from the side, never from above or behind. For safety reasons, bathroom wall lights must be controlled by a pull cord.
*The End of Day Lighting Company.*

**Left** Simple downlighters like these shown left are a good choice for a period-style bathroom.
*R & S Robertson Ltd.*

**Below** In a modern room, lighting can be concealed behind a timber or tiled baffle.

## Lighting the Bathroom

The days of the spartan, all-white bathroom illuminated by a chilly fluorescent glare are, fortunately, over. Modern sanitaryware comes in soft, warm colours, such as peach, champagne and cream, usually with tiles to match. Bathrooms today are usually carpeted, heated and comfortable. Lighting should be planned both to complement this relaxing atmosphere, and to provide good illumination around mirrors where clear light is needed for making-up and shaving.

## Safety First

Before planning bathroom lighting, there are certain safety regulations which must be followed.

* Electricity and water do not mix (water is a good conductor), so conventional light switches cannot be fitted in the bathroom. The option is a pull-cord switch (safe because your wet hand cannot come into contact with the switch itself), or a switch on the wall outside the bathroom.
* Wall lights must be of a type specially designed for bathroom use and must be controlled by a pull-cord switch. Your electrician will advise.
* Track and spot arrangements are not suitable for bathroom use.
* The only socket allowed in a bathroom is the type specially designed for use with an electric razor. It is dangerous to use any sort of plug-in lamp, heater or hairdryer in the bathroom.

**This page** Wall lights come in styles to suit most period bathroom suites — and can be effectively used with modern sanitaryware, as shown right.
*R & S Robertson Ltd.*

### General Lighting

Downlighters recessed into the ceiling are ideal for bathroom use. The number of lights you use depends on the beam angle of the fitting and how large an area it can illuminate. In the bathroom, the effect of light is enhanced by the reflection from the shiny finish of mirrors, sanitaryware and tiles. This can produce a rather cold look, especially if the colours are mainly pale. But a cold effect can be avoided if you use recessed ceiling-mounted, spill-ring fittings with gold reflectors.

Interesting aspects of your bathroom decor (such as a large plant, a display of shells, a picture or even the bath itself) can be highlighted with narrow-beam downlighters. Use wide-beam downlighters in conjunction with these to give a good background of general light.

**Below** The wall-hanging is highlighted with two narrow-beam, directional downlighters. Used in conjunction with wide-beam downlighters they provide a good general light. *John Cullen Lighting.*

**Right** This clever modern scheme uses fluorescent lighting concealed behind a baffle to light the basin area (mirrored to make the room look larger), combined with downlighting. *Executive Bathrooms.*

### Task Lighting

Task lighting in the bathroom really means a well-illuminated mirror. For a good, clear view the light should come from the sides of the mirror, never from above it or from behind the user.

There are many mirrors on the market (mostly from Europe), fitted with integral lights positioned to give the very best illumination.

Many also have a heating element so that the glass does not mist over. Some combine the roles of mirror and bathroom cabinet.

An alternative to buying this sort of custom-made fitting is to make your own arrangement. Tungsten lights, fitted at the sides of the mirror, give a good, flattering light (avoid fluorescent light as it tends to give the healthiest person a pale, drawn look). All purpose-made bathroom lights are suitable.

A Hollywood-style row of bulbs at either side of the mirror is a time-honoured arrangement — but can look rather overwhelming! This brash effect can be avoided by using low-wattage, crown-silvered bulbs instead of the ordinary plain or pearl type.

Tungsten strip lamps are another alternative but they do not look particularly attractive and it is best to conceal them behind a pelmet, so that the mirror has the appearance of being recessed into a frame.

**Above** A Victorian-style wall light is the perfect complement for this traditional bathroom.

**Left** Modern bathroom furniture usually includes light fittings, positioned to illuminate both the mirror and the room.

## CHAPTER 3

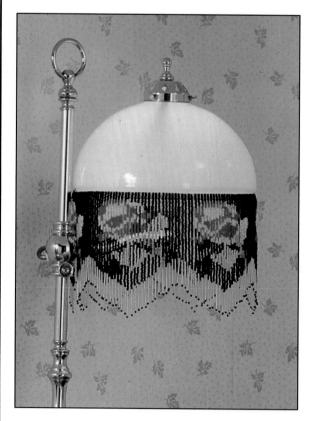

**Above** Beaded lampshades can be obtained in many designs and colours and are perfect for a traditional Victorian-style bedroom. *Christopher Wray's Lighting Emporium.*

**Right** Bedroom lighting should be soft and subtle, so combine table and wall lamps with downlighters controlled by dimmer switches. Bedside and wall lights should be controllable from the bed. *Adrian Sankey.*

Lighting bedrooms is much easier than lighting areas of the home that are used throughout the day and evening. There are fewer criteria to take into consideration — the main requirements for a bedroom are good light for dressing in front of a mirror, as well as for putting on make-up, and subdued light, controllable from the bed, for reading.

In a busy family, where the main living areas of the house are always a hive of activity, the bedroom can become a private retreat, a place to sew, read, work or simply think in peace, a fact well worth considering when you are planning your lighting. Adding a work or relaxing area can be simply a matter of installing a table or a comfortable chair and a plug-in light, but there are other possibilities.

**General Lighting**

There is a great temptation simply to install a central ceiling pendant in the bedroom in the vague hope that it will do as general lighting. In reality, the pendant light is of no practical use as it creates shadows rather than the soft level of light best suited to the bedroom environment.

As in most other rooms in the house, halogen downlighters provide the best general light. Because general light in the bedroom need not be as intense as in living areas, you will not need quite so many fittings. In an average small bedroom, four downlighters combined with one uplighter, plus a bedside lamp, a lamp next to the mirror and, perhaps, some wardrobe lighting will be more than adequate.

Wide-beam sources give the softest general light in the bedroom. Remember to take the colour scheme into account when choosing lights. Less light is needed if the room is in a pale, reflective colour, more if it is dark. Downlighters can double as accent

**Right** This bedroom is brightly lit when all the fittings are in use. However, when the pendant fitting is switched off the room takes on a much more relaxing feel. *Christopher Wray's Lighting Emporium.*

**Below** This subtle, relaxing effect is achieved by combining bedside lights with ceiling-mounted dimmers. *John Cullen Lighting.*

lights in the bedroom, and you can use a directional fitting to display a picture. Set wide-beam eyeball fittings into the window recess to show stylish curtains to advantage; set wall washers in front of wardrobes to light them from top to bottom (and to help you see what is inside when you open the doors).

It is a good idea to control general lighting with dimmers, positioning switches beside the door so that the lights can be turned on when you go into the room. As you will probably switch the lights out, relying on bedside fittings for reading in bed, there is no need to fit second controls so that you can switch off the main lights without getting up.

### Bedside Lighting

A good bedside light, which will allow one partner to read without keeping the other awake, is a bedroom essential. Almost any sort of lamp will do, but choose one where the on/off switch is easy to reach, and which allows room on the bedside table for books, spectacles and other odds and ends.

Ideally, the light should shine onto your book, but not into your eyes. Judging whether the lamp you have selected will have this effect can be rather difficult, but as a general rule, a small to medium fitting with a conical shade will give the right effect.

An alternative to bedside table lamps is to have lights built into the wall just above the bedhead. The lights should have integral controls to make switching on and off easy, and they should not project too far from the wall otherwise anyone sitting up suddenly will hit their head on the shade. One of the best types of light for this is the 'decorator's classic', a simple shade on an extending brass arm which can be pushed back against the wall when not in use.

Think about bedside lamps in terms of the overall design scheme used in the bedrom. Shades can be

**Below** This lamp was originally intended for use with candles, but there are specialists who can convert this sort of design to electricity — making it perfect for bedroom use, as can be seen (right). *The R.B.C. Trading Co Ltd.*

**Left and far left** Where a bedroom is large and splendid, or where fabric and window treatments are particularly elaborate, keep lighting simple. Large, fussy bedside lamps or ceiling fittings would be out of place in either of these rooms. *Cohen & Pearce Period Interiors; Sue Stowell Fabrics & Wallpapers.*

co-ordinated with curtains or bedlinen, or you can choose pretty Art Nouveau designs, where flower heads of opalescent glass are set on curved brass stems. Candlestick lamps are ideal for bedside use. They are narrow enough not to clutter the bedside table and tall enough to spill light just where it is needed. If the bedroom is pretty and traditional in style, look for lights which reflect this. China oil lamps converted to electrical use look delightful in a pretty, cottagey room; look for Tiffany styles if the look is Victorian or Edwardian, for simple, modern ceramic crackle bases in a comfortable modern environment.

If your choice of style is high-tech, then small, narrow-beam directional fittings are a good choice for mounting above the bed. This sort of fitting has the great advantage of restricting light to a narrow area, which is ideal for a couple where one partner likes to read late while the other sleeps.

**Lighting Mirrors**

Unless you are lucky enough to have a dressing room, you will need to think about lighting the mirror in the bedroom. The best way to light a mirror is from the sides, never from behind or from the top.

It is unlikely that you will want to spoil the intimate atmosphere of the bedroom with Hollywood-style bulbs at either side of the mirror, or with fluorescent strips. If the mirror is on a dressing table, light it with small, pretty table lamps at either

**Right** An opulent lamp for a
Victorian or Edwardian-style
bedroom. *Antique Decor,
Melbourne, Australia.*

**Below** If you have invested in a
stunning window treatment, show it
off with carefully-positioned lighting.
*John Cullen  Lighting.*

side. A tall cheval mirror can be lit by positioning it
between two directional downlighters, or close to a
small lamp table.

### Wardrobes

It is well worth lighting your wardrobes as it makes
life so much easier — there can be nothing more
frustrating than peering into the dark recesses of a
wardrobe, attempting to locate a favourite garment
in the gloom.

If you have fitted wardrobes, lighting can be
incorporated when they are built, or can be added
later. This sort of lighting works on the car courtesy-
light principle. When the doors are opened, a small

**Left** Modern fitted furniture does
not always allow room for bedside
lights, so fit wall lamps above the
bed instead.

**Below** Elaborate Art Nouveau
designs mix well with modern cane,
old pine or polished wood.
*Christopher Wray's Lighting Emporium.*

switch is released and the light comes on.

Lighting the interior of large, traditional or
antique wardrobes is much harder, and easiest to
achieve by using a directional downlighter.

**Children's Rooms**

As your child grows, from baby to toddler,
through the years under ten to the teens, his or her
lighting needs will change. Babies and toddlers need
simple, general lighting, backed up with a night
light. Children between five and ten need task
lighting for play; teenagers need an arrangement
which caters for homework, hobbies, entertaining,
dressing and listening to music.

**Below** This charming little night light is one of the very first electrical fittings made with children in mind. *The Lamp Gallery.*

**Left** These illustrations of 'The Non-glare Bed Light' are taken from a lighting catalogue of the 1930s and are typical of the period. *Dernier & Hamlyn Ltd.*

The nursery, as such, was a Victorian invention. Before that, children simply had rooms, rather than a special space adapted to their needs. In most prosperous Victorian families, the whole of the upper floor of the house was given over to the children and their nursemaids. Often, these apartments were far from comfortable — as R.W. Edis points out in his book, *The Decoration of Town Houses*, published in 1881:

'In the dreariness of town houses, nothing has struck me as so utterly cruel as the additional dreariness which generally pervades the rooms devoted to children — the nurseries of the house, the rooms in which our little ones spend so large a portion of their early lives...'

Tucked away in their dark, often gloomy apartments at the top of the house, Victorian children rarely enjoyed the benefits of artificial light. The gas might be lit for tea on winter evenings, but it was only very lucky children with caring parents or a kindly nurse who were allowed to have a night light. Early night lights were small stubs of candle, sometimes held in a perforated china holder, or afloat in a dish of water so that the child could not touch the flame. Later models were of glass and made in the shape of animals and birds. The candle fitted inside and gave out a friendly glow.

Small Victorian oil-fired night lights with a base in the shape of an animal or bird (owls were popular) and a glass chimney with a shade above, succeeded the candle. Examples can still be found at reasonable prices, and make a delightful collection — too valuable alas to be used for their original purpose.

Parents today are less inflexible than the stern Victorians, and modern children who cannot sleep without the comforting glow of a light have plenty of choice. Some of the nicest night lights around are life-size geese, ducks, rabbits and cats in opaque

**Right and below** Choose bedside lamps to complement fabrics used on the bed. Ceramic bases, made either from antique vases, as shown right, or in simple modern shapes, below, can be combined with plain or patterned shades. *Cohen & Pearce Period Interiors; Mr Smith Interiors.*

creamy white plastic (the bulb is safely contained inside and gives a low, comforting glow); china cottages, filled with Beatrix Potter families of rabbits or mice, fairy mushrooms and men in the moon: a comfort to even the most nervous child.

Fairly new to the lighting market are glow friends, toys which light up when the child cuddles them. These can be a safe alternative to the plug-in light if your child is the adventurous type who might be inclined to pull a plug-in light off the bedside table. Safety is a vital consideration when choosing a night light for a toddler. The bulb must be safely enclosed, so that the child cannot touch it and burn his or her hands — or, worse still, remove it from the socket while the power is still on.

An inexpensive alternative to a nursery night light is a plug light. This looks just like an ordinary 13 amp plug but lights up when pushed into the wall socket.

One of the nicest night light ideas I have ever seen was in an old beamed cottage in Oxfordshire. The owners had strung miniature white Christmas tree lights along the angle between the beam and the ceiling, giving a comforting twinkle for their toddler who was afraid of the dark but inclined to dismantle conventional night lights.

Always connect lights by using a safety plug which cannot be pulled out by a child. When the light is unplugged, fit a safety cover over the socket. Toddlers love pushing sharp objects into electrical sockets — with disastrous consequences.

General lighting for a room used by a baby or toddler can come from either an overhead pendant controlled by a dimmer (so that if the child cries during the night, you can use a dim light, much less likely to cause a sustained bout of wakefulness than bright light), or from an array of recessed down-lighters. Pendant lights are, in many ways, more attractive in a child's room. There is now a good choice of children's shades available, with many featuring favourite nursery characters and also working as mobiles. You could make your own shade (see the instructions for simple gathered shade in the section on making your own lampshades), and hang miniature toys from the edge of the frame.

Once children reach the age of three or four, when colouring-in and painting become of interest, you will need to add task lighting. There is no better choice than an adjustable arm fitting, clamped either to a shelf above the work area, or to the edge. Light can be directed where it is needed, and the fitting will serve your child's needs well into the teenage years.

Bedside lighting will also need to be changed as the child grows. Older children like to read in bed, and will need a bedside lamp which gives a better level of light than a night light. Bunk beds must be lit individually, so that one child can read while the other is asleep. Wall-mounted angle-arm fittings are a good choice.

Because older children spend a lot of time playing on the floor, bright, general light is essential. Ceiling-mounted wide-beam spotlights, mixed with one or two narrow-beam spotlights which can be directed onto hobby or work areas to boost task lighting, are the best choice.

## CHAPTER 4

**Above** Garden lighting can be a feature in its own right — as shown by this impressive glass and lead globe. Outdoor lighting specialists can provide lights designed to be a part of garden design, as well as a source of light. *Illawarra House, Toorak, Melbourne, Australia.*

**Right** Floodlighting is used to draw attention to this impressive statue, while the background lighting is provided by tungsten-filament bulbs positioned along the eaves of the house. *Leslie Walford, Sydney, Australia.*

Carefully planned lighting adds a new dimension to the garden, allowing you to enjoy it by night as well as by day. Garden lighting serves two purposes: it is both practical and creative. Practical lighting around doors, garages, steps and pathways is important for safety and security. Creative lighting emphasizes and enhances interesting garden features, such as pools, hanging baskets, statuary, summerhouses and trees.

**Safety First**

There are safety rules which must be obeyed when installing lighting outdoors.

* Use fittings specially designed for outdoor use. Damp and the fact that the user is in direct contact with earth can lead to fatal accidents if the fittings are not weatherproof.

* Fittings should be protected by a residual current circuit breaker. This is a device which cuts the power off instantly if there is an earth leakage fault. Ask the electrician to fit RCCBs when the lights are installed.

* Check the condition of all outdoor cable regularly. (Rodents sometimes chew it.)

* Always switch off the current at the mains before replacing bulbs or carrying out other maintenance work on outdoor installations.

* Garden lighting can be run from either the mains (essential for complex arrangements), or from a complete lighting kit using lights on spikes connected to a low-voltage transformer (these kits are available from garden centres). The transformer connects to the mains supply via an ordinary 13 amp socket (the garage is an ideal place to put it). Flex supplied with the kit connects to two 12 volt terminals on the transformer itself. This sort of lighting is suitable for DIY installation, but follow the manufacturer's instructions carefully. Check the flex periodically and renew it if the PVC insulation is damaged.

**Right** This rooftop garden has been designed using strong, simple plant shapes, displayed in interesting planters, all highlighted by use of cleverly positioned halogen downlighters. *Leslie Walford, Sydney, Australia.*

**Below** If a house is in a remote area or has a long driveway it is worth installing security lights. The more sophisticated systems are activated by sensors and light up when the building is approached. *At Home.*

**Below** Another view of the rooftop garden, showing how floor-standing spotlights highlight the collection of white flowers and the tall plants beyond. *Leslie Walford, Sydney, Australia.*

## Practical Lighting

Rummaging for keys on a dark door step is both dangerous and, if the weather is wet or cold, uncomfortable. A light beside the front door gives the house a welcoming look, and means that would-be intruders cannot lurk unseen.

The traditional doorway lights are a couple of coach lamps positioned to either side of the doorway. Garden centres and lighting specialists stock a good selection of these. It is important to make sure that the one you choose gives a good, bright light (some emit a feeble yellow glow which defeats the object of buying a lamp) and that is suitable for outdoor use.

Choose a lamp which suits the style of the house. A large lantern would, for instance, look out of place beside a cottage doorway but quite acceptable on a larger house. Think about the period of your home too. If the house is modern, look for a plain, well-designed lantern or bulkhead-style light. It is a sensible idea to have the switch fitted with a timer, so that the light can be set to come on as soon as darkness falls and switch off again when it is daylight.

For safety's sake, all dark areas around the house should be lit. A bulkhead-type fitting above the garage door, beside the dustbins or wherever you feel at risk, is usually sufficient.

If the house is in a remote area, a badly-lit street, or has a long pathway or drive, it is worth thinking about installing more sophisticated security lights. These are activated by a sensor and will switch on as soon as anyone approaches the building. Most modern systems cannot be accidentally activated by animals. A specialist security lighting company should be consulted before installing such a system.

Flights of steps, either down from a patio or where the garden changes level, should always be lit. If

# OUTDOOR LIGHTING

**Right and below** Outdoor lighting can combine decoration with practicality. Period fittings are as effective in lighting a dark corner as modern, purpose-made security lights. *Sugg Lighting Ltd; R.J. Chelsom & Co Ltd.*

there is a wall at either side of the steps, this can be done with bulkhead fittings. If not, choose **PAR 38** outdoor spotlights directed onto the steps, or globe or mushroom fittings on a spike. (PAR spotlights have bulbs with reflectors to direct a strong beam of light, and are therefore particularly well-suited to outdoor use.) Lights on spikes can be positioned at intervals up a long path or driveway. If the garden is large enough, and the house is period in style, Victorian street lamps can look very effective.

Originals, converted to electricity, can be found at architectural salvage specialists. Larger garden centres stock reproduction models.

**Creative Lighting**

Look at your garden carefully and make a lighting plan before you contact a specialist installer. The plan should show all the areas where you want security lighting, and the areas where you want to use lighting for effect.

Some garden features are obvious choices. Statuary, a sundial or a bird bath can be bathed in light from a PAR 38 spotlight. Beds of flowering or interesting foliage plants can be illuminated by a PAR wide-beam spotlight on a spike. The advantage of this is that the light can be moved around when other plants come into flower.

Hanging baskets or a small balcony can be lit by PAR 38 spotlights positioned on the ground. If you have a row of baskets, or some boxes positioned on top of a wall, light them with PAR 38 floodlights.

There are two ways to light trees. One is to shine light up from the ground, using a PAR 38 spotlight. The other is to festoon the tree with strings of lights. This works best in the winter when the tree is bare.

PAR 38 spot and wide-beam lights fixed to trees or walls can be directed to give general illumination of flower beds, walls or architectural features.

Outdoor lighting is intense and the glare can be dazzling, so choose fittings with louvres or cowls to

**Below** This indoor pool house is lit by both wall lights and underwater lighting. Underwater lighting alone is not enough when the pool is indoors. Even outdoor pools must have some perimeter lighting — which must be left on at night so that there is no danger of anyone falling in.

**Left** Submersible lights specially made for pools are the best way to show off a water garden. Bulbs can be plain white or coloured. Submersible lights must be fitted by a qualified electrician. *Sydney, Australia.*

prevent too much glare.

Think, too, about lighting the house. Floodlighting need not be reserved for stately homes and castles. It looks just as effective on a small house, especially if it stands back from the road in a country area where there is no competition from street lighting. Wide-beam PAR 38 fittings are suitable for the average house — your electrician will advise on where they should be positioned to flood the building with light. Very large buildings need specialist floodlighting.

**Pools and Ponds**

The shimmer of water illuminated by submerged lights looks wonderful at night. Swimming pool lights should be fitted when the pool is installed — it is very difficult to do this afterwards. Fish ponds are much easier to deal with as there is a wide range of submersible lights available at garden centres.

Submersible floodlights come two or three to a single track and can be angled to illuminate different areas of the pool. They work well with an evenly shaped pool, but inevitably leave some areas dark if the pool is an irregular shape. Circular, submersible lights are more flexible as they can be floated at different levels (by weighting the cable joining the lights with stones) and positioned just where they are needed.

**Right and below** A garden which is quite unremarkable by day can become dramatically interesting at night — simply by positioning lights, such as spotlights on spikes, to highlight attractive plants, trees and features.

When planning pool lighting, always position lights to either side of the fountain, so that the moving water sparkles in the light.

Pool lights are available plain or coloured. Plain lights tend to give a more natural effect. In addition the edges of the pool can be attractively lit if you highlight luscious plants with PAR 38 spotlights.

**Entertaining**

If you are having a barbecue, the glowing charcoal will provide some light, supplemented by garden lighting if you have it. Atmosphere can be added with garden flares, and with candles. Both of these have the added advantage of warding off mosquitoes.

Garden flares are rather like medieval rushlights and come in tall versions, for sticking into the ground, or in small pots. Dot the tall versions around the garden (keep them well away from overhanging branches or you may cause a fire). Use the pot lights on low walls and close to the eating area.

The table can be lit by candles. Protect them from the wind by putting them in tumblers or wine glasses (secure the candles to the bottom of the glass with a blob of melted wax). Two or three candle glasses of different sizes look attractive grouped together. If you have a wide glass salad bowl, half fill it with water. Float night lights on the surface, and push small flowers such as nasturtiums, pansies, freesias or daisies between them. Use night lights with metal bases as they float better.

Stand a grouping of different-sized candles on a piece of mirror (stick the candles to the mirror with melted wax). The light from the candles is reflected back by the mirror, giving a pool of illumination around the dining area. This idea can be used indoors too.

Weatherproof Christmas lights designed for outdoor use are another way to bring light and colour to outdoor eating. Drape the lights around the branches of a tree, or string them across the patio. But never risk using indoor lights outside as there is a great danger of electric shock. Always use a residual current circuit breaker (RCCB) when using plug-in lighting outdoors.

**Left and above** This clever idea is an ideal way to light a conservatory or indeed any other room. The Pot Light Company will install the light fitting and paint any design of your choice, from trailing ivy to a teddy bear holding a honey pot, onto the surrounding wall. *The Pot Light Company.*

## CHAPTER 5

# VISUAL TRICKS

**Above and right** Using a lighting projector allows you to frame pictures in light. Projectors can outline even quite complicated shapes, but you will need help and advice from a skilled lighting designer. The collection of Lalique glass, shown right, is cleverly displayed by being lit from behind. *John Cullen Lighting.*

Everyone has something to show off — be it a priceless or simply prized collection, or even a flourishing houseplant. Light is invaluable in making the most of any sort of display, bringing out the beauties of glass, ceramics, stone, wood and of living foliage.

**Plants and Flowers**

Well-positioned light enhances the colours of leaves and flowers, casts interesting shadows on walls and ceilings, and can help to keep plants healthy.

All plants need light, but just how much depends on where the plant comes from. Ferns and other woodland dwellers need very little light; cacti, succulents, flowering plants and those whose natural habitat is the canopy of a tropical rainforest, need far more — in some cases up to 16 hours a day. Plants will, of course, survive in dim light — but they will not thrive, so if you want to keep a display located away from windows healthy, some sort of lighting is essential.

Any sort of light is suitable for accenting a display of flowers, but tungsten sources show colours at their best. Light can come from a directional spotlight, or from a semi-recessed ceiling fitting. These fittings are also suitable for displaying plants normally situated in good light once darkness falls. If you want to encourage plants which spend their day away from a strong source of natural light to grow, you will need to introduce a special grow-bulb. Grow-bulbs provide the mixture of red, infra-red and blue essential for the production of chlorophyll (the colouring-matter of the green parts of plants). Grolux tubes and bulbs are available in a variety of sizes, from 15 to 65 watts, and can be used in normal fluorescent fittings. They are not, however, particularly decorative (the light given off is bluish),

**Below** A combination of directional, low-voltage downlighters, and a drum uplighter positioned to shine through the leaves of a flourishing palm, give this room a dramatic feel. Lighting like this does not just happen — it needs careful thought and planning.
*John Cullen Lighting.*

**Left** A ceiling-mounted, directional downlighter has been used to illuminate this embroidery with clear white light. You could achieve a similar effect with a spotlight.
*John Cullen Lighting.*

nor are they controllable, so they should only be used if essential.

Directional tungsten or tungsten-halogen light beamed from a ceiling fitting is, of course, the simplest way to light plants. For best effect, position either a single large plant, or a display of smaller ones beneath a narrow-beam, ceiling-mounted spotlight or a recessed downlighter. Very large plants can also be lit from below by using a drum-shaped uplighter. These are not particularly attractive to look at, but can be concealed by the plantpot. Move the uplighter around until the light casts a really interesting shadow pattern on the walls and ceiling.

Small, low-growing plants can be clustered around a table lamp, or displayed on glass shelves lit from below by small directional fittings. An already attractive effect can be greatly enhanced by positioning a mirror behind the greenery.

When lighting plants, you must remember that light bulbs give out heat, which can easily frizzle tender leaves. It is, therefore, important to check the leaves nearest to the light after it has been on for about an hour. If the leaves are warm, either move the light, or introduce a cool-beam low-wattage spotlight or a dichroic multi-mirror bulb.

### Paintings and Sculpture

Forget the traditional brass picture light if you really want to show art to its best advantage. Galleries, whose livelihood does after all depend on display, never use these fittings for the simple reason that they are ineffective, lighting only the top section of the picture. A properly-angled, ceiling-mounted directional light illuminates all of the picture evenly.

Lighting a picture can prove complicated, and throws up the old chicken and egg situation. Which do you do first — hang the picture then install the lights, or hang the picture, taking existing lighting into consideration? If it is possible to plan lighting initially with pictures in mind, you are obviously in an advantageous position. To light a picture well, the light source needs to be placed between the person looking at the picture and the wall. The fitting should be far enough away for the beam to cover the picture, but not so far that people can cross the beam. A good rule of thumb for directional fittings is to position them at about 1 metre (40 inches) from the wall. Make sure before you buy the light that it can be tilted to the angle needed.

Once you have the light, an easy way to check the position before final fixing is to wire it up to a long lead. Switch it on and experiment with the angle until you find a position which offers the minimum of reflection combined with maximum illumination. If a problem with too much reflection is unavoidable, you can have the picture fitted with non-reflective glass. Specialist picture framers can supply this.

**Right** Make the most of tall, dramatic plants by lighting them so that the shadow of the leaves adds interesting patterns and shapes to a blank wall. Using a drum uplighter, either positioned on the floor, or on a small table close by, is the best way to do this. *John Cullen Lighting.*

Very large canvasses or wall hangings will probably need light from more than one fitting. The beams from the fittings should cross one another on the surface of the picture or hanging, so that no area is left in shadow.

Pictures or hangings acquired well after lighting has been planned need not be condemned to a life of insignificance. Miniature plug-in low-voltage uplighters, called highlights, can be positioned below the painting or sculpture to beam light onto it. These fittings are incredibly versatile; they come fitted with their own transformer and allow the bulb to be tilted to different positions. A wide-beam bulb fitted in a highlight will effectively light a large picture. A narrow-beam bulb will direct a dramatic and intense light onto a sculpture or piece of china. A similar effect can be achieved with plug-in eyeball spots on flexible arms, but these fittings are rather obtrusive for a traditional interior.

Collections of china or glass displayed in an alcove or on a low table can be lit in exactly the same way as pictures. The most effective treatment for single large pieces is to position them beneath a narrow-beam ceiling fitting. But, in either case it is equally possible to use highlights as an alternative.

## Something Special

In galleries you may have seen pictures, sculptures and ceramics illuminated so that the object seems framed by the light. This effect comes from the use of a framing projector — a specialist (and rather expensive) piece of equipment, and only really worth considering if you have something really spectacular to display.

A framing projector is a low-voltage fitting available in suface, track or recessed designs and containing an arrangement of frames and shutters. These can be positioned to shape the light beam to the size of the object it is directed at. This has the result of making pictures appear to be lit from behind; it is a spectacular treatment for large, unframed modern works.

Lighting specialists can cut masks to fit inside projectors so that a sculpture or large vase can be outlined in light.

The positioning of a framing projector is crucial if the fitting is to create the right effect. Most manufacturers provide instructions, but a good electrical shop should be happy to advise. Make sure that you do know the exact size of the picture or object to be lit, before you go to buy the projector.

However, it is important to be very careful when lighting old or valuable pictures and textiles. Museums usually limit the lighting of oil paintings to a fairly low level for the simple reason that too much light can cause damage. In the home, objects are likely to be lit for much shorter periods, so the strength of bulb is not quite so crucial. But heat from bulbs can be eliminated by using low-voltage or dichroic multi-mirror bulbs.

**Left** Cleverly designed fittings are used here to display pictures, light the chessboard on the small table in the centre of the room, and provide general light. Carefully positioned table lamps add interesting shadow patterns from the plants. *John Cullen Lighting.*

## Visual Tricks

One of the principal attributes of light is that it can be used to create all sorts of interesting effects that alter the look of a room, and the sense of space. Theatre designers are experts at the art of the illusion, with the skill to make small spaces seem large, to create perspective and moving shadows. A few simple techniques will make light an important part of the decorative scheme and open up a world of interesting possibilities.

## Theatrical Effects

Modern lighting technology allows many special techniques used in the theatre to be brought into the home. One of the simplest tricks to steal from the stage is to fit spotlights with coloured filters to change the atmosphere of the room.

Blue filters, used on spotlights in conjunction with the clear, white light of downlighters create a dramatic, moody effect. Coloured filters are available for most spots and are inexpensive. Experiment with colours and effects until you find something you like. Possible colour additions are a blue spot directed onto a display of glass, a green spot onto plants or a pink spot to create a warm corner.

More complex effects can be achieved by using theatrical projectors, rather like framing projectors, to beam colours and shapes onto floors and ceilings. Light is put through a mask, called a gobo in the theatrical world, which is cut out to outline a particular shape. You could, for instance, project a pattern of leaves onto walls behind a plant, or clouds or a moon and stars onto the ceiling (lovely in a bedroom). Colour can be added too, so the light can have a gentle, tonal tinge to make the effect even more interesting.

If you are really ambitious, look for a motorized projector, and create a moving image. It is then possible to have clouds, birds or whatever you choose progressing slowly across the ceiling or walls. This, needless to say, is an effect which works best on a high, plain ceiling, or flat walls painted in white or a light colour.

**Right** Using coloured lenses in spotlights adds a subtle shading of pink and blue to the shadows from the leaves of this large plant. *John Cullen Lighting.*

Rows of small bulbs set into clear tubing can be used to bring a touch of Hollywood glamour. Set them into the edge of stairs, hang them side by side like beaded curtains or run a strip of them along cornices or around doors. This is an effect which works best in a modern, minimalist home.

### The Art of Expansion

Cleverly used, light can make a room seem larger — a trick well worth knowing where space is at a premium.

The wrong way to make a small room look larger is to light it with clear, white light, so that all the boundaries are clearly defined. All this does is to make it clear that the space really is small. Instead, the secret is to paint the walls and ceiling of the room in a pale colour. A tinted white is ideal, as it has the effect of softening the lines which mark the limitations of the space. Lighting should be designed to make the space seem undefined — a mixture of angled light and shadow can give an impression of movement and freedom.

Ceilings can be made to seem higher by using uplighters. In a small room, drum-shaped uplighters, which can be concealed behind furniture or plants, are best — it is essential to keep clutter to a minimum where space is limited. Use wall washers to bathe flat areas of wall in soft light. Accent architectural features with downlights or directional spotlights.

Mirrors are, of course, a time-honoured way to make small spaces appear larger. Used in combination with lighting, mirrors can double the visual impression of both space and light.

The cardinal rule when using mirrors and light together is never to shine the beam directly into the mirror as the effect of this is to produce a blinding glare. Two mirrors placed opposite each other will

**Left** Directional spotlights are a flexible way to highlight plants, pictures and interesting furniture or features. Make sure that the lights are positioned so that they flood the object with light — too near or too far away and the whole effect is lost. *John Cullen Lighting.*

**Overleaf** In the days of Edison and Swan the only choice in light-bulbs was either the bayonet or screw fitting in just one size. Today, however there are dozens of different light sources all giving different effects at different levels. *GTE Sylvania, USA.*

widen a narrow room. A mirrored wall at the end of a square room will make the area seem twice as long, and looks particularly effective when plants are grouped in front of the mirror and lit from above.

Floor-to-ceiling mirror used at right angles to a window will double the amount of natural light. At night, the same effect can be achieved if you fit recessed downlighters into the ceiling at about 1 metre (3 ft) from the mirrors.

Mirror set into alcoves, lit by directional spotlights positioned at right angles, can give the impression that there is another room just beyond. Arch-shaped pieces of mirror can be used in the same way — but make sure that the mirror reflects the whole of another object. A display of plants lit by an uplighter is particularly effective, giving the impression that the room leads into a garden beyond.

**Thinking Big**

Large spaces involve just as many lighting problems as smaller areas. Bright, overall light will make a large room seem chilly and unwelcoming. The answer is to break the space up by creating visual focus, accenting a sofa, a low table displaying a collection of family pictures, an architectural feature, a group of seating, pictures, the fireplace or a sculpture.

These sources, used in conjunction with good general light from downlighters and wall washers will make even the largest room seem comfortable. Fit controls so that it is possible to isolate certain areas; you can then have an intimate, well-lit seating area around the fireplace, with the rest of the room dim, brightened here and there by accents on pictures or other displays.

## CHAPTER 6

# UNDERSTANDING LIGHTING

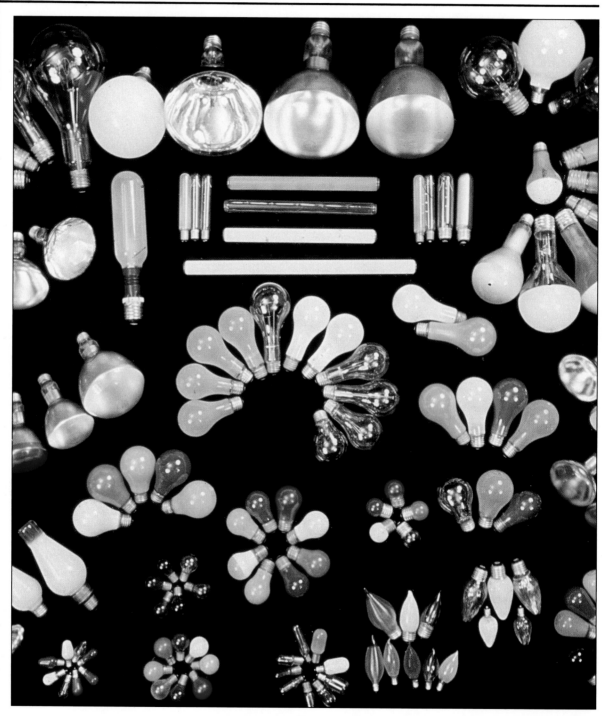

Light is vital to human well-being. Scientific studies have shown conclusively that lack of sunlight is associated with depression.

In the home, lighting is both a necessity and a way to make living conditions more comfortable and attractive. Thanks to Thomas Edison and his invention of the light bulb, we now have instant light on tap, and the technology to create an enormous range of different effects, from the subdued light of early dawn or dusk, to the brightness of a summer day.

There is more to lighting than being able to see in the dark. A good, well-planned lighting scheme is as much an asset to your home as attractive decoration. Good lighting can be used to enhance the beauty of a prized painting or piece of sculpture, to bring out the colours in a rug or wall hanging, to create a soft, relaxing atmosphere, or a clear, practical light for working.

Modern light fittings make it possible to create an interesting scheme very easily. There is no longer any need to rely on the time-honoured combination of a ceiling pendant and one or two table lamps. Today's recessed ceiling downlighters mean that some areas of the room can be bright while others are dark. Beams can be directed just where they are needed, or can even be designed to outline an object in light. Accent lights can be used to create warm pools of light — around a favourite chair, for instance, or above a dining table. Modern task lights can be angled to shine on sewing or homework — no more working in your own shadow. Wall washers and uplighters allow you to use the reflective qualities of the walls and ceilings. It's rather like being an artist but instead of using a brush and paint as your medium you have the controllable technology of a world of light fittings at your disposal. However, the average modern lighting shop is rather like an Aladdin's Cave, with every sort of fitting imaginable on show. The consumer, faced with this bewildering choice, must decide on fittings most suited to his or her needs. But with the general lack of helpful advice on lighting in many shops, it is possible to be quite unaware of the potential of certain fittings and the drawbacks of others. How fittings can be made to work successfully in a room is another difficulty most consumers will face. This chapter aims to dispel the confusion and offer imaginative and practical advice.

## Low-voltage Lighting

Once confined to offices, low-voltage lighting is now widely available for domestic use. Low-voltage fittings operate on a 12 or 24 volt supply (instead of the usual 240 volt mains). The power is reduced by a transformer. Both bulbs and fittings are small and unobtrusive, but give a clear, white light, ideal for illuminating paintings, sculpture or tapestries. Tungsten-halogen bulbs are best, and come in 20 to 75 watt versions, giving a variety of beam angles. Multi-mirror low-voltage bulbs (known as dichroic) have an integral reflector. This means that heat from the bulb goes backwards, rather than forwards into the path of the light, with the result that there is no danger of over-heating a delicate painting or tapestry. Bulbs can be changed at will — there is no need to install a new fitting if you decide one day to fit a larger wattage bulb with a wider beam angle. Recessed, eyeball, semi-recessed and spotlight low-voltage fittings can all be found in specialist lighting shops, but installing these low-voltage light systems is not a job for an amateur — they must be fitted by a qualified electrician.

## Eyeball Fittings

An eyeball is a variation on the downlighter. The fitting is semi-recessed and can be swivelled to direct light as required. This can be very useful in a room where there is a need to mix accent and general light, as some of the eyeballs can be directed while others are left pointing downwards. Because eyeball fittings can be swivelled, a system can be installed and eyeballs can then be directed as required. This system also means that if you decide to change the lay-out of a room you can adjust the lighting accordingly, without having to dismantle the existing system.

Eyeballs and downlighters cannot be fitted in every ceiling. Depending on the particular light fitting a space of between 10 cm and 30 cm (4 in - 12 in) is needed between the ceiling and the floor above. The ceiling must be in good condition. Crumbly old lath and plaster ceilings are usually unsuitable. In addition, recessed fittings cannot be used on a solid ceiling.

**Pendant Fitting**

A pendant fitting is the type which hangs down from the ceiling. Pendants are most commonly used for centre lights, but central lighting is never a very satisfactory form of illumination. It tends to be too dazzling, and to cast too harsh a glare. A combination of wall lights and ceiling-recessed downlighters is much better than a mix of a centre light and wall fittings.

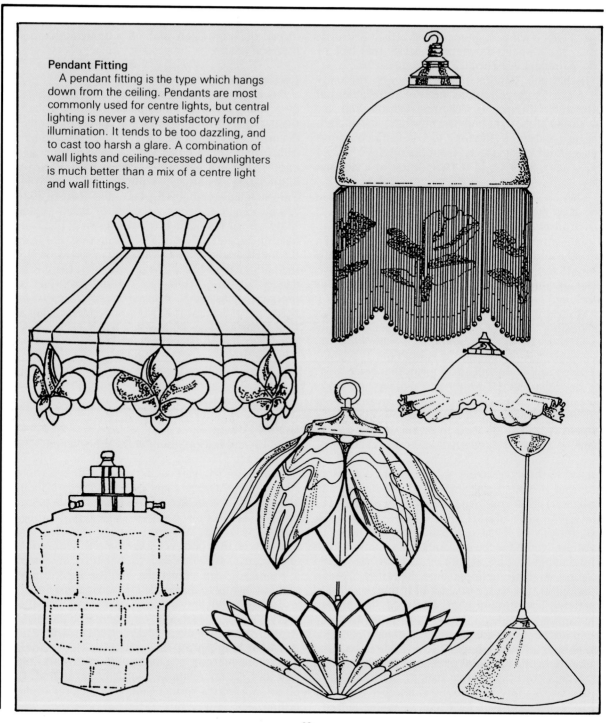

## Rise-and-fall Fittings

A rise-and-fall is a pendant light which can be raised and lowered by pulling on the shade. The main use for rise-and-fall fittings is to illuminate the dining table. When the light is lowered, it casts an intimate glow over diners and food but can be raised to cast a wider light. These fittings vary from simple devices, where the pulley mechanism is concealed inside the ceiling rose, to complex period-style designs featuring visible pulleys and counter-weights. Their versatility makes them a popular choice for kitchen tables and dining rooms.

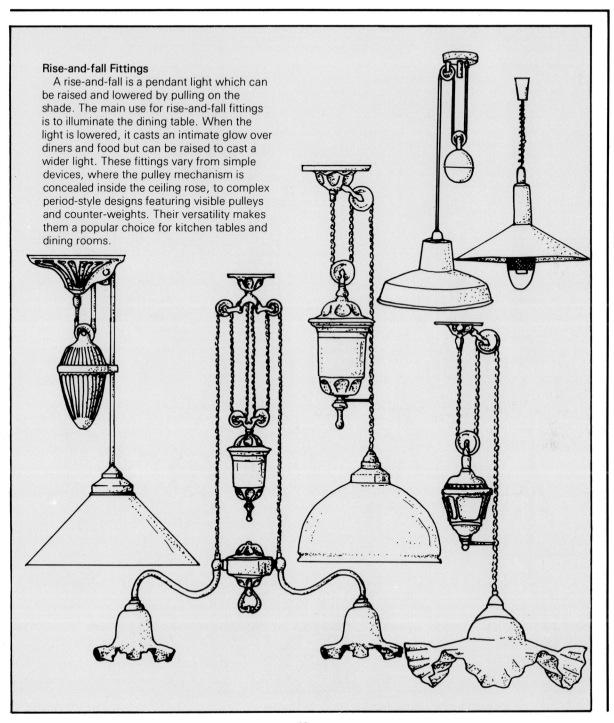

### Decorative Pendants

Lights featuring several bulbs, chandeliers, ornamental oil lamps and lanterns, and other fittings attached to the ceiling by a rigid tube, are all termed decorative pendants. Their use as a centre light in a living room or bedroom can prove limiting as they give a flat, uninteresting light. Oil lamps and lanterns can, however, be very useful and look good in a traditional hallway, or above a scrubbed pine kitchen table. They are full of character and add an unusual touch to the most conventional of rooms.

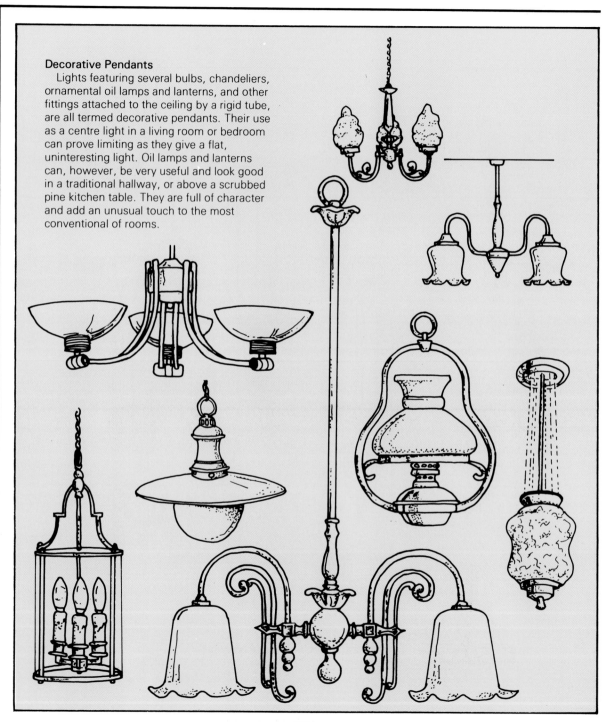

## Accent Lights

If you want to light a picture, a plant, a table or a collection, some form of accent light is needed.

At the very simplest level, an accent light can be a simple plug-in table or standard lamp casting a pool of light down onto a polished table top, a chair or a collection. Table and standard lamps come in an enormous range of styles, from ultra-modern, sculptural designs to traditional brass, wood or ceramics. The lamp in its own right plays an important part in the decorative scheme and it is, therefore, important to choose lamp bases and shades that will match the period of the house, or the style of the furnishing.

Directional eyeball fittings and ceiling-mounted spotlights on a track can also be used as accents, but be careful how you use them. Ideally, the beam should cover just the object it is intended to highlight, and should not strike other parts of the room. Directional ceiling-mounted lights are far more effective for lighting a picture or a wall-hanging than the traditional brass picture light — and, in addition, they are much less obtrusive.

Before fitting any sort of directional accent light, make sure it really can be tilted to the angle needed.

## Task Lighting

A task light is not a special fitting in itself. The term is used to refer, quite simply, to any sort of light with a purely practical purpose. Task lighting can be used to illuminate flights of steps, or a doorway at night. Office-style directional task lights are invaluable for reading, writing or sewing. A standard lamp positioned behind and slightly to the side of a favourite chair makes the perfect reading light. Almost any sort of fitting will do — providing that it casts the right sort of light and in exactly the right spot for the task in hand.

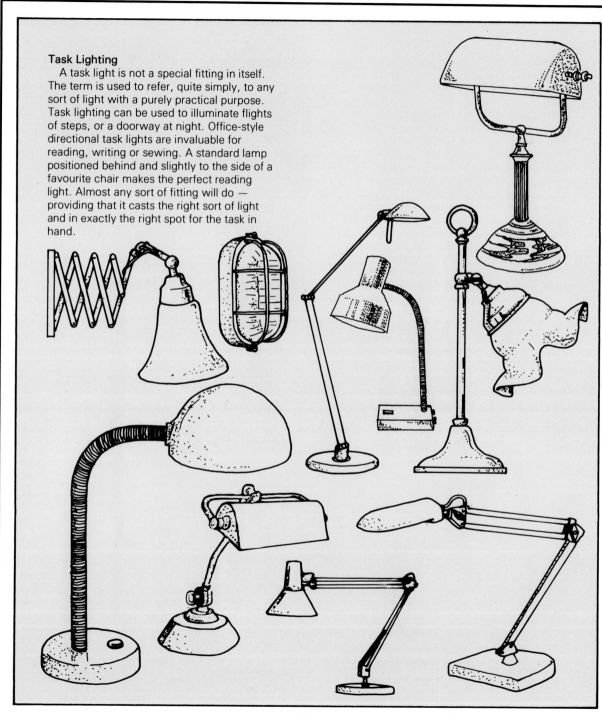

## Downlighters

A downlight is, as the name suggests, a fitting designed to beam light downwards. One downlight will illuminate a fairly small spot in the room, but a collection of them, spaced across the ceiling, provides extensive background lighting. Downlighters can be surface-mounted (this type is useful for positioning above a sideboard or console table), or they can be partially or wholly-recessed in the ceiling.

They are either fitted with reflector bulbs, or incorporate their own reflectors so that the light is directed downwards. Lights with built-in reflectors are more expensive, but will work out cheaper in the long run as the bulb costs less than a reflector bulb. They give a better beam too, so you may decide that the additional cost is worthwhile.

Downlighters are fitted with either silver or gold reflectors. Silver does not affect the colour of the light; gold gives a warmer glow which can be useful in a bathroom where the combination of white light and white tiles or sanitaryware tends to produce a rather chilly effect.

Wall lights, where the shade directs the beam downwards, are another form of downlighter. They are useful as a method of casting a pool of light over a sideboard, a small table, a chair or other piece of furniture positioned below or slightly to the left or right of the fitting. The type with a flexible brass arm, hinged at the centre, are more versatile than fixed designs.

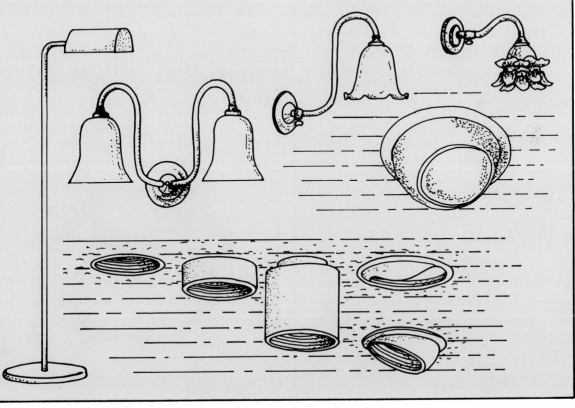

## Wall Washers

Ceiling-mounted wall washers direct light across vertical surfaces. They cast a soft, warm light over a wide area, and are particularly effective where walls are painted in pale colours as the light is reflected back into the room.

Groupings of pictures, architectural features, wall hangings or shelves of books can all be lit by carefully-positioned and angled wall washers which bathe a wide area in light.

Wall washers come in a variety of shapes and sizes but all have some sort of reflector shaped to direct the light so that it covers the wall. They use the same type of bulbs as downlighters together with tungsten-halogen. It is possible to buy wall washers to match downlighters.

To work well, wall washers should be positioned at about 1 m (3 ft 3 in) from the wall. The maximum distance between fittings should be around 2 m (6 ft 6 in). But you can reduce the number of fittings by half if you use tungsten-halogen bulbs which are far more efficient than GLS or reflector bulbs.

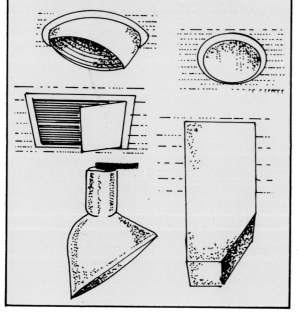

## Close-mounted Lights

A close-mounted light means one fitted directly to the ceiling with a backplate holding the bulb (or bulbs). The main use for close-mounted lights is in bathrooms and toilets, and water-tight versions are used for showers. Bulkhead lights are a wall-mounted variation and they are mainly used outdoors but can work very well in, for example, a high-tech kitchen.

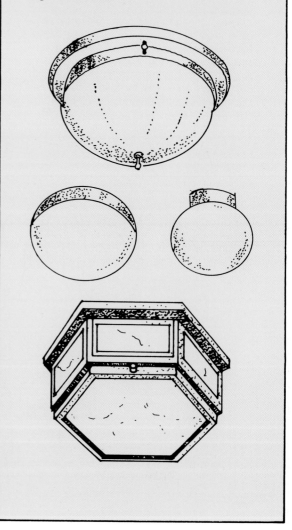

## Uplighters

Uplighters direct their beam onto the ceiling, and have the magical effect of making any room seem instantly higher and more spacious. They can emphasize the graceful proportions of a classical room, highlighting elegant cornices, and can equally give an impression of height in a low-ceilinged room.

Uplighters can be either wall-mounted, floor standing or suspended from the ceiling. A small uplighter hidden on the floor behind a large plant is particularly effective and casts dramatic shadows over walls and ceilings. Although it is possible to buy half-sphere wall-mounted uplighters fitted with ordinary light bulbs, their effect is limited, although they do look attractive and modern plaster versions can be painted to match the walls of a room. Washing the ceiling with light is an effect that can only really be achieved by choosing lights fitted with tungsten-halogen bulbs.

Tungsten-halogen bulbs are, as their name suggests, filled with halogen gas. When the tungsten filament is heated electrically, a reaction takes place which results in a bright, clear white light from a fairly small bulb. Combined with a reflector, a 300 watt tungsten bulb can flood an average sized ceiling with light. All halogen bulbs give off a lot of heat, so be careful to position the light at least 1 m (3 ft 3 in) from the ceiling and be sure to keep the beam away from anything inflammable, such as a draped, tented ceiling.

Halogen bulbs can be dimmed, but when dim their light reverts to yellow.

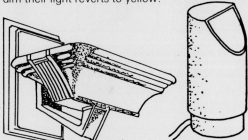

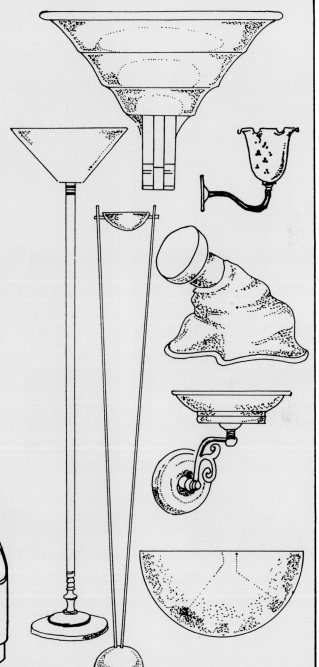

A central ceiling light casts shadows on the page and is not the most suitable source for reading or sewing.

A reading lamp should be positioned behind and slightly to one side. This also applies to a bedroom lamp which should either be placed on the bedside table or mounted on the wall just above the bed. However, excessive contrast is a strain on the eyes so the lamp should be supplemented by soft background lighting which will illuminate with reduced sharpness of contrast.

It is a good idea to have a low-level indirect light near the television set as this will reduce eye strain.

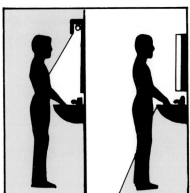

In a kitchen, a central light alone is not enough as it will cast shadows over the work surfaces.

A good solution is to fit strip lights under wall units, concealed behind a baffle, although these may reflect in polished surfaces, so raise or lower the light to give a better reflecting angle.

Light mirrors from the side and not from above, but avoid lights which will reflect in it.

Long dining tables will need more than one pendant fitting unless it is supplemented by downlighters.

Take care when choosing a pendant lamp for a dining table. If the bulb protrudes below the shade fit a crown-silvered bulb to avoid dazzling the diners.

A rise-and-fall fitting can be adjusted to suit the diners. The light can then be positioned at the right height to avoid dazzle, but high enough not to obscure the person opposite.

Cupboards or shelves can be lit by a directional downlighter. Alternatively, interior cupboard lights can be controlled by a switch operated by the opening and closing of the door, using the same principle as the car courtesy light.

Avoid a light that throws your own shadow onto the page. The best solution is to use a concealed light in the same way as lighting a kitchen work surface.

An adjustable lamp provides good illumination and, when supplemented with soft background lighting, will reduce eye strain.

# UNDERSTANDING LIGHTING

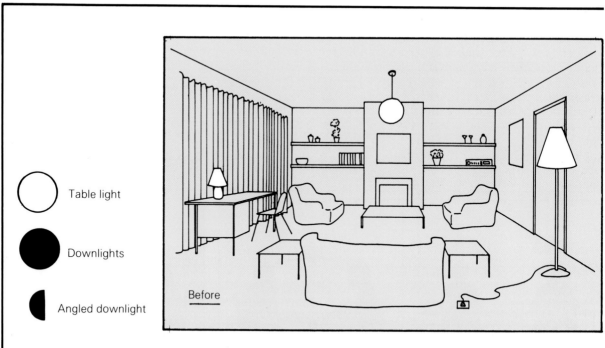

Table light

Downlights

Angled downlight

Before

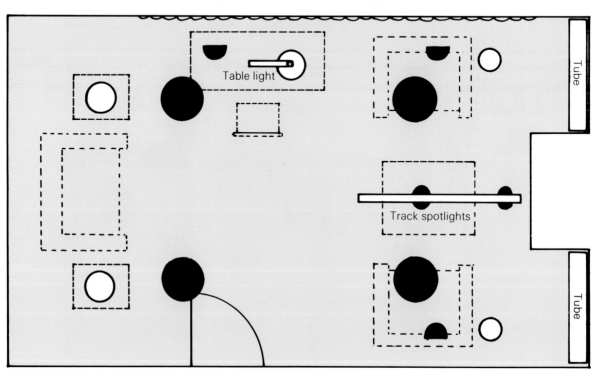

Table light

Track spotlights

Tube

Tube

Nowadays, the family living room in most homes has many roles, from study and playroom to library and entertainment centre. It is a complex area to light so careful thought must be given to the lighting scheme to accommodate all these functions. The plan shows a typical room with a three-piece suite, desk and occasional table. In the 'before' illustration, the central pendant light concentrates interest in the middle of the room and makes it difficult to read because you are facing the light source. The standard lamp will improve matters a little but the trailing flex can be dangerous and the lamp on the desk is too small to be of any real help. In the 'after' illustration, general light is provided by down-lighters which have been connected to a dimmer switch. Accent lighting is provided by spotlights on a track, which replace the central pendant. Angled downlighters or eyeball fittings emphasize the pictures and curtains, and tungsten tubes have been fitted behind pelmets on the shelving units. Two large table lamps at either end of the settee complete a scheme that can be adapted to all types of needs.

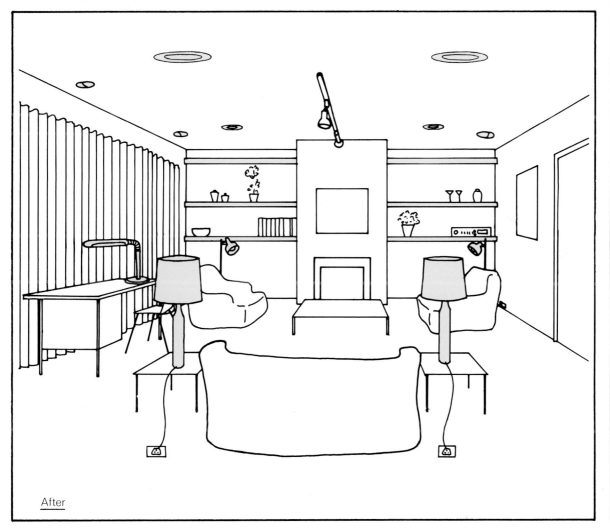

After

1. Wire stripper — can be adjusted to cut through insulation only without damaging the covering of the wires inside.

2. Pliers — with insulation handles and wire-cutting jaws.

3. Long-nosed pliers — useful for manipulating wires in confined spaces and for making loops at the ends of cable.

4. Cable slip — used for fixing cable and flex to walls, skirtings and joists.

5. Torch — always keep a torch beside the fuse box to give light when replacing fuses.

6. Cartridge — keep a selection of different weight fuses available.

7. Fuse wire — available on cards with a variety of different weights of wire.

8. Electrician's screwdriver — long thin shaft to reach into confined spaces. It is useful to have one for both types of screw — cross-headed and slotted.

9. Mains tester — small screwdriver with insulated shaft and handle. There is a neon bulb in the handle which lights up when touching a live terminal.

10. Sharp knife — useful for cutting cable, but should not be used for removing insulation from cables. Always use adjustable wire strippers to avoid damage to the covered wires inside.

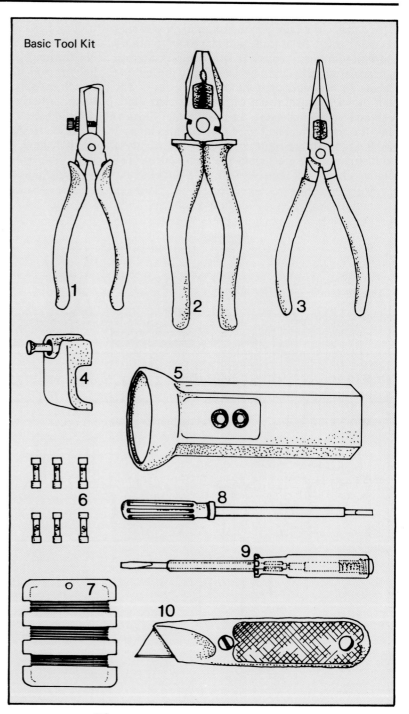

Basic Tool Kit

## Safety First

● Before doing any work which involves revealing bare wires (replacing a light switch or a ceiling pendant, for example), switch off the power at the fuse box and remove the circuit fuse. If you are not sure which fuse controls the circuit you are working on, keep the power off until the work is finished.

● Always disconnect plug-in fittings from the mains before doing any work on them.

● Have electrical work done by a reputable electrician, preferably one who is a member of the NICEIC (National Inspection Council for Electrical Installation and Contracting).

● If you intend to do a lot of electrical work in the house (replacing all the light switches or ceiling roses for example), invest in a mains tester. This lights up if it touches a terminal or wire which is still live.

● If a fuse blows persistently, it could indicate a major wiring fault. Call in a qualified electrician. Faulty wiring can easily cause a fire.

● Never run cable under a carpet, or coil long lengths of it behind furniture. It may overheat.

● Never, ever use an electrical appliance in the bathroom, other than a shaver connected to a proper two-pin shaver socket.

● Bathroom light switches should be out of reach of anyone using either the shower or the bath, so pull-cords must be used.

Never treat electricity casually. It is dangerous stuff. A simple mistake can very easily cause death or at best a severe shock. Stay safe by following these simple rules.

Before you attempt any ambitious lighting plan, it is important to ensure that the wiring in your house is suitable for the scheme that you have in mind. All homes need extra wiring for fittings such as low-voltage recessed lamps, but in some cases a completely new system may be needed.

Electricity enters your home via the consumer unit, sometimes called the fuse box, but which is really three boxes, one of which is the sealing chamber where the service cable from outside enters. This box contains the main fuse. This is the property of the electricity board and can only be worked on by them. The purpose of the fuse is to stop the whole neighbourhood being plunged into darkness should your circuitry develop a serious fault. If the electricity board decides that the circuits in your house are dangerous, they can remove the fuse until things are made safe. Another cable connects the sealing chamber to the electricity board's meter, which measures the amount of power you are using.

Thick red and black cables lead from the meter to the consumer unit or fuse box. This box contains fuses, which protect the circuits in the house from overloading. For example, if an appliance which needs a much heavier fuse — such as an electric fire — is plugged into a lighting circuit with 5 amp wiring and fuse, the fuse is designed to melt and break the circuit. These fuses can come in several different designs.

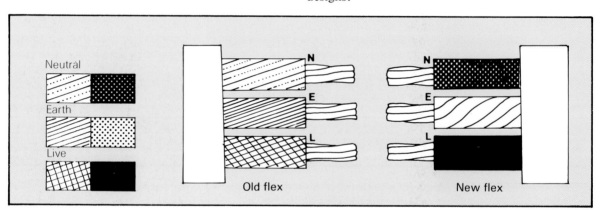

Neutral

Earth

Live

Old flex        New flex

**What the colours mean**

Old flex — black is neutral, green is earth and red is the live wire.

New flex — light blue is neutral, green and yellow striped is earth and brown is live.

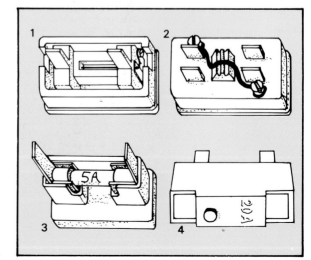

1. Protected wire fuse. 2. Wire bridge fuse. 3. Cartridge fuse. 4. Miniature circuit breaker (MCB).

### Wire Fuses

Wire fuses have a porcelain body and two or four prongs. They can be repaired by fitting new wire of various thicknesses (depending on the rating of the fuse). The wire is connected to a terminal beside the prongs and either runs through a tunnel across the fuse carrier, or over the top. Lighting runs on 5 amp fuses, so lighting fuses should always be repaired using 5 amp wire. If fuses keep blowing then there is obviously a problem with one or more appliance, and unless you can isolate the cause yourself an electrician should be called.

### Cartridge Fuses

These fuses are fitted with a cartridge, rather like the sort found in a 13 amp plug. Lighting fuses are normally fitted with white cartridges. If the fuse blows, simply replace the cartridge. Keep some available just in case.

To identify the blown cartridge, check fuses with a metal-cased torch. Take the end cap off the torch. Touch one end of the fuse to the battery with the other end resting on the metal casing of the torch. If the torch lights, the fuse is working.

### Miniature Circuit Breakers

The latest type of fuse is the miniature circuit breaker or MCB. These are well worth paying extra for when having your home rewired. If a fuse blows, a small button on the front of the cartridge pops out.

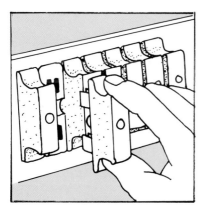 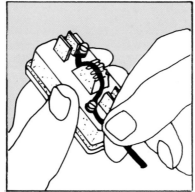 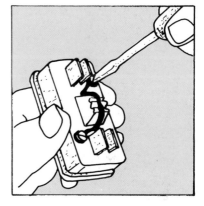

To repair a blown fuse first turn the power off at the mains. Check all the fuses until the blown one is found. Remove the blown fuse. If, however, your system is fitted with MCBs, a small button on the front of the fuse will have popped out. In this case simply push the button back in.

Remove the old cartridge or broken wire. Fit a new cartridge or replace the wire by wrapping new wire clockwise round one screw and tightening the screw to hold the wire in place.

Draw the wire across the bridge or, in the case of a protected fuse, thread it through the hole and wind it clockwise around the other screw. Tighten the screw. **Remember — it is essential to use the correct cartridge or weight of wire as a fuse designed for higher power can allow wiring to overheat and cause a fire.** Replace the fuse and turn on the power.

All you have to do is push it back in.

To mend a blown fuse first switch off the power, then remove the fuse. (It may be necessary to remove more than one until you find the burnt-through wire.) Replace the wire with wire of a similar weight, but remember that it is dangerous to use wire of a lower or heavier loading than the type needed for the fuse. If the wire is too thin the fuse will just blow again, but a fuse designed for higher power can allow wiring to overheat and cause a fire.

**Inspecting the System**

Knowing whether you are wiring a safe modern system or an unsafe, old-fashioned one, is a simple matter of observation. If you have two or three fuse boxes instead of the normal one (and sometimes a second if you have electric central heating) attached to a board beside the meter, and carrying old-fashioned porcelain fuses, have it replaced. It is sometimes very difficult to know what is what in this sort of box and there is a danger that you could be working on a live circuit without knowing it.

Another pointer is the cable. If the lighting cables are of the modern plastic-covered type then the system has been rewired, but if it is old-fashioned plaited fabric or rubber covered then it is an old system and should be replaced.

**Circuits**

Examine cabling where it runs through the loft or

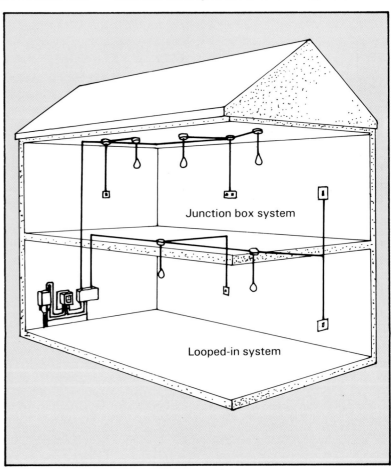

Junction box system

Looped-in system

under floorboards. If it is of the old-fashioned, rubber-covered type, or if there seem to be a large number of circular junction boxes, replacement is necessary. Similarly, if sockets are of the round pin type, then the system is hopelessly out of date and should be replaced at once. Switches should be in good condition, that is, free from any cracks. If any switch or socket becomes warm when in use it should be replaced. Sockets and switches must not spark when used.

## Lighting

If there are three wires inside lampholders, the lighting circuit needs replacement, especially if you are intending to run modern fittings.

Rewiring is never cheap, but it is essential if you intend buying expensive fittings for an ambitious lighting plan. In most cases, an old system simply will not take either the fittings or the load. However, complete rewiring is not a task that an amateur should undertake. Remember that all wiring must be approved by the electricity board before they will connect up to the sealing chamber. If the job has been done badly, approval will not be forthcoming. Always use a qualified electrician, either from the electricity board or from a reputable company.

Although it is not wise to attempt major electrical jobs unless you are absolutely certain of what you are doing and are familiar with IEE wiring regulations, there are some simple tasks safely within the

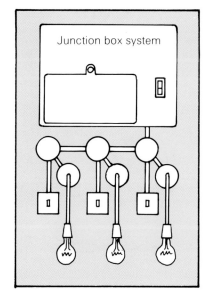

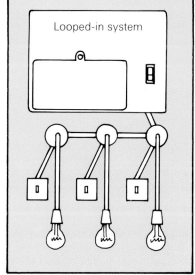

Older lighting systems will be of the junction box type. In this case the supply cable is taken to a junction-box before being run to the ceiling rose.

Modern systems use the 'looped-in' system where the cable is run from the consumer unit to the first ceiling rose. The cable for the next ceiling rose is looped-in to these terminals, as are the switch wire and the wires to the pendant; the same happens in succeeding roses.

scope of the average handy person. However, before attempting any of the following tasks it is essential to switch off the power and remove the fuse for the circuit while you work. The power can be switched back on again while the fuse is out, but must be switched off when you return the fuse to the box.

### Rewiring a Pendant Lampholder

A damaged pendant lampholder can be dangerous, especially if the fitting is old. Check lampholders from time to time and replace cracked ones. Dismantle metal holders to make sure that the earth wire is still attached and that the terminal is free from corrosion.

**Plastic lampholders** are far more common than the metal type and have a threaded skirt section that screws onto the fitting which is attached to the end of the cable. They are only suitable for use with a two-core flex. On old wiring systems, you may have a three-core flex for lighting. In this case, use a metal lampholder.

**Metal lampholders**, most commonly found on old lighting systems, have three connectors. A metal holder must never be used with a two-core flex, or in a bathroom or other steamy area.

### Replacing a Ceiling Light or Rose

Replacing a pendant ceiling light with a new fitting needs no special skills. However, replacement with recessed or close-mounted ceiling lights is more

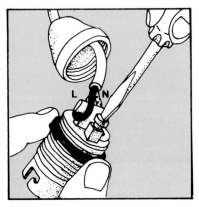

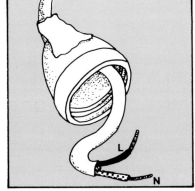

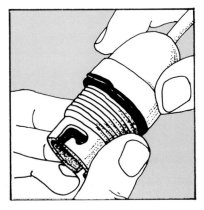

To rewire a pendant lampholder, first switch off the power. Remove the circuit fuse. Switch on again. Unscrew the cap or retaining ring from the lampholder. Slide the holder up the ceiling flex so that you can see the terminals (where the ends of the cable are connected to the fitting). Loosen the terminal screws and pull the wires out.

Check the condition of the wire. If it is broken or brittle, cut back until you reach a sound section. Strip a little of the covering from the ends of the wires. Slide the cap part of the new fitting up the cable and secure with a piece of plastic tap until needed.

Fit the live (brown) wire and neutral (blue) onto the terminals, and twist the wire around the two lugs at each side of the holder. Tighten up the terminal screws. Slide the cap back down and screw in place. Check that the flex hangs straight. Replace lampshade and bulb.

complicated and should only be carried out by an amateur who is skilled at dealing with electrical installation and who has a full knowledge of electrical regulations. If this is not the case, it is safer to consult a qualified electrician.

The power should be switched off at the consumer unit (main fuse box). Switching off at the wall is not enough. Unscrew the ceiling rose and make a note of how the existing cable is wired in. It is important to determine if the system is new or old. If there is only one red and one black cable, the system is of the old junction box type. On a modern loop-in system, there will be three sets of red and black cables (two for the circuit, one for switching), plus three yellow and green earth wires, as shown in the illustration. If the system is very old and you cannot identify the wires, call an electrician.

Identify the switch cable with a piece of tape and then disconnect the wires from the terminals. Separate any which are twisted together, but identify what they are with tape. (If this is not done it will be difficult to know what to connect to where.) The old backplate can now be unscrewed and removed. Use a screwdriver to knock out the entry hole in the new backplate and thread the cables from the ceiling through it. The new backplate can now be fixed to the ceiling and the wires connected as they were before. This accomplished, the pendant for the new light you are fitting can be threaded through the hole in the centre of the new cover and the cable

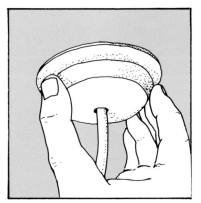

To fit a new ceiling rose turn the power off at the consumer unit (main fuse box). Unscrew the ceiling rose and make a note of how the existing cable is wired in. If you cannot identify the cables, replace the cover and call an electrician.

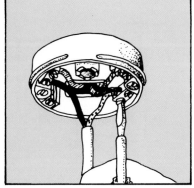

Remove the two-core lampholder flex and disconnect the wires from the terminals. Identify what they are with tape. If you don't do this, you will find it difficult to know what to connect to where.

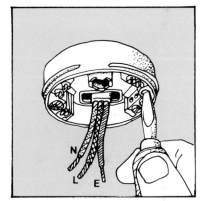

Straighten the mains wiring and separate any twisted together. Unscrew the old backplate and remove.

connected as before. If you are connecting a large light fitting rather than just a ceiling rose and lampholder, it helps to have someone else holding the light fitting while you do this. Screw the cover firmly onto the backplate and then switch the power back on.

These instructions will also apply if you simply want to lengthen the cable to suspend a pendant lamp over a low side table or dining table.

**Lenthening a Lamp Lead**

The cable supplied with lamps is often far too short, especially if you are rather short of sockets. Lengthening cable is a simple process. You will need two or three-terminal flex connector, depending on the number of wires inside the flex. An alternative to using a flex connector is to use a small in-line switch which works in much the same way. Disconnect the existing cable from the plug and strip a little insulation from one end of the new cable (which must be of the same type as the old). Connect the live (brown) wire from the old cable to one side terminal, the earth, if used (green and yellow) in the middle and neutral (blue) at the other side. Do the same with the stripped end of the new cable, connecting the wires of the same colour into the corresponding terminal. Screw the connector cover in place. Attach a plug to the other end of the cable.

In the case of an old lamp which still has the original wiring intact, it is essential that the wiring is

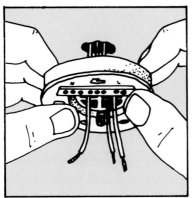

Use a screwdriver to knock out the entry hole in the new backplate. Thread the cables from the ceiling through it. Fix the backplate to the ceiling. Connect the wires as before.

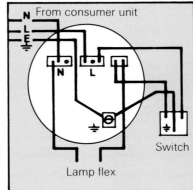

Thread the lampholder flex through the new cover and screw the flex into the correct rose terminals. Replace the cover and switch the power back on.

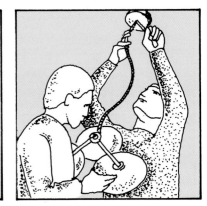

These steps also apply in the case of a new pendant fitting such as a chandelier where the rose cover is usually supplied with the fitting. However, it helps to have someone else supporting the fitting for the last stage.

replaced from the lamp itself as the covering to the wires has probably perished and is therefore unsafe. Disconnect it from the lamp, noting carefully how it was wired, and attach new cable.

**Wiring a Plug**

Knowing how to wire a plug is essential if you want to have any form of free-standing lighting. It is a simple job — although a surprisingly large number of people do not know how to do it. The standard plug in use in the UK is the square, three-pin 13 amp model. In a very old house which has not been re-wired, there may be two or three-pin round pin models and these should be replaced as soon as possible. Before you begin, make sure that there is

enough cable exposed to connect the lamp to the plug. To strip cable, you will need a sharp knife and a cable stripper. Make a nick all around the flex at about 2.5 cm (1 in) from the end, being careful not to cut into the coloured wires underneath the outer covering and pull away the outer covering. Using cable strippers, strip away about 12 mm (½ in) from the end of each coloured piece of cable. Twist the filaments of metal in each piece of cable together to make firm ends. Take the cover off the plug by first undoing the large screw in the centre, then the two smaller ones. Lift the two halves of the plug apart. Continue turning the two smaller screws until there is sufficient room to slide the cable easily under the cord clamp. If the plug has a spring cord clamp (two

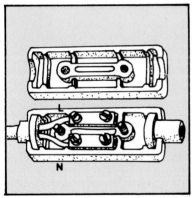

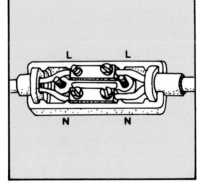

To lengthen cable on a lamp you will need a two or three terminal flex connector, depending on the number of wires inside the flex. Remove the plug and thread the cable from the lamp through the connector, fixing the live (brown) wire to one side terminal and the neutral (blue) wire to the other. (If the wiring on the lamp is old or damaged it must be replaced. Disconnect the cable from the lamp, noting carefully how it was wired, and attach new cable.)

Strip a little insulation from one end of the new cable (which must be of the same type as the old) and thread it through the other end of the connector fixing the wires to the corresponding terminals. Screw the connector cover in place and fit a plug to the new cable.

pieces of plastic at angles on either side of the hole where the cable enters the plug), you will not need to do this. Lift out the fuse. Connect the brown (live) wire to the terminal beneath it, either by undoing the screw, wrapping the end of the brown wire around the terminal post, then doing the screw up again, or by undoing the screw, pushing the end of the brown cable through a small hole in the terminal and doing the screw up again, depending on the type of plug. Connect the other wires in the same way. If an earth (green and yellow) wire is present it goes up the middle. Neutral (blue) goes to the left. Tighten the screws of the cord clamp over the cable until it stays firmly in place. Put the cover back on the plug and tighten the central and smaller screws.

A new development in plugs is the snap-fastening terminal. Here wires are held by small locking clips and there is no need to undo the terminal screws. Simply lift the locking clip, insert the wire then let the clip go.

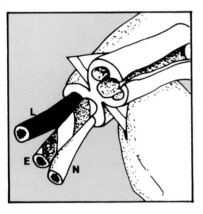

**Wiring a plug**
Make a nick all around the flex about 2.5 cm (1 in) from the end, being careful not to cut into the coloured wires underneath the outer covering. Pull away the outer covering.

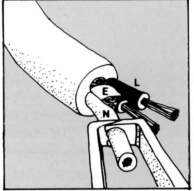

Using cable strippers, strip away about 12 mm (½ in) from the end of each coloured piece of cable. Twist the filaments of metal in each piece of cable together to make firm ends.

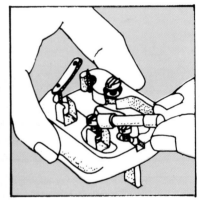

Open the plug by undoing the large screw in the centre. Loosen the screws of the cord clamp and remove the screw complete from one side so that the clamp can be moved to one side. If the plug has a spring cord clamp (two pieces of plastic at angles on either side of the hole where the cable enters the plug) this will not be necessary. Remove the fuse.

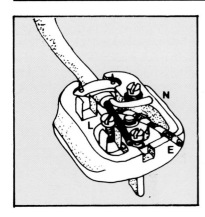

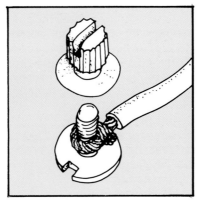

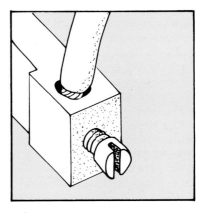

Connect the brown wire to the terminal beneath the fuse. Connect the other wires to the relevant terminals. Earth (green/yellow) goes up the middle. Neutral (blue) goes to the left.

If the terminals are of the screw type, remove the screw and wrap the end of the wire clockwise round the terminal. Re-tighten screw to hold in position.

If the terminals are of the block type, loosen the screw and insert the ends of the wire into the hole. Tighten the screw to grip wire firmly.

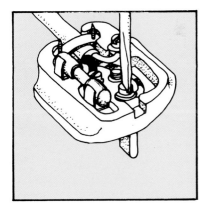

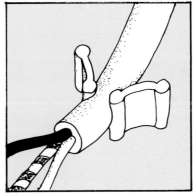

Replace the cord clamp over the cable and tighten the screws until it stays firmly in place. Replace the fuse. Make sure that there are no loose strands of wire and replace the cover.

If the cord clamp is of the spring clip type just push the flex between the two pieces of plastic. This grip holds the flex firmly when under tension.

### Putting up Spotlight Tracks

Replacing an overhead pendant fitting with a spotlight track is a reasonably simple job — but check first that the power cable from the existing overhead light is suitable for use with a spotlight track. If in doubt, check with an electrician.

The first important point to consider when fitting a track is the position of the track. Make sure that the lights will not hamper the opening of cupboard or room doors, and use a pencil to mark the fixing points for the track. Isolate the electrical circuit you are working on by removing the fuse from the fuse box, and then drill holes through the marked fixing points. Insert wall plugs, then screw the track in place. Feed the power cable into the terminal box at the end of the track. Connect up the system following the manufacturer's instructions which will be given with the track. Replace the cover of the terminal box and slide spotlights onto the track.

Switch the power back on and angle the spotlights as needed. As well as the wide variety of spotlights available for use on a track it is possible to buy a variety of fittings for pendant lights. This is very useful if you want to suspend two low pendants over a long table.

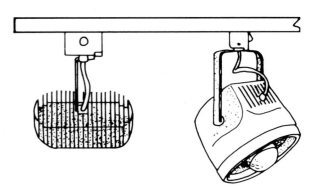

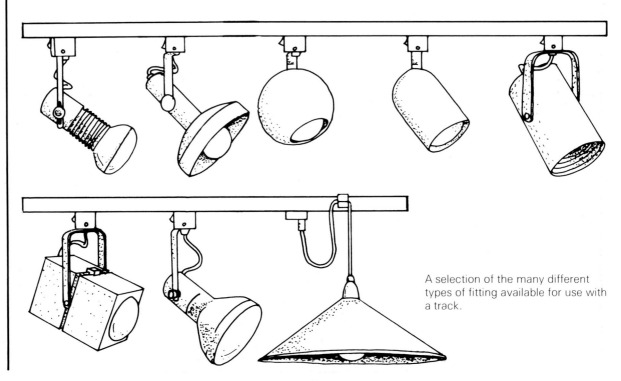

A selection of the many different types of fitting available for use with a track.

Single circuit track

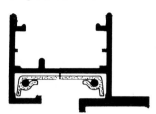

Multiple circuit track

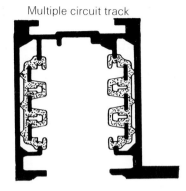

**Left** Tracks are obtainable as single circuit systems, which work on single switching systems, or as multiple circuit systems, with up to four lines which can be activated separately giving much more versatility and greater lighting potential.

**Below** These illustrations demonstrate some of the possible light-falls obtainable from track spotlights, including (bottom left) a framing projector.

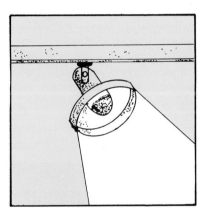

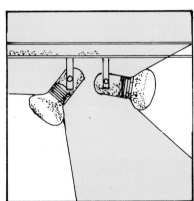

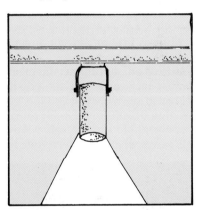

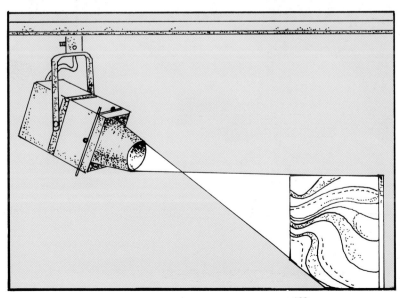

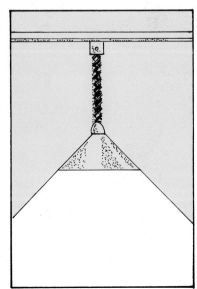

## Types of Bulb

Light bulbs have come a long way since the days of Edison and Swan, when the choice was either bayonet or screw fitting in just one size. Today, there are dozens of different light sources, all giving different effects at different levels. The source of light and the type of bulb are the two most important aspects of choosing lighting — the actual appearance and style of the fitting is secondary.

There are three main types of light source for use in the home.

## Tungsten-filament Bulb

The tungsten-filament bulb, also sometimes called the GLS (general lighting service) or incandescent bulb, was Edison's invention and is still the biggest seller in home lighting. When the electricity is switched on, the tungsten filament glows through the bulb, which can be of clear, pearlized or tinted glass. A recent development in GLS bulbs was the introduction of soft tones, bulbs tinted to give an almost imperceptible rose or soft yellow glow. These are attractive when used in bedside lights.

The light given by tungsten is close to natural light, making it especially suitable for domestic use. Tungsten bulbs need no special transformers, but have a short life and are not particularly energy efficient. Nor are they flexible enough to be used for special lighting effects.

## Types of Tungsten Bulb

Tungsten bulbs come in several varieties. Conventional bayonet or screw fitting types for use in pendant lights and table lamps come in sizes from 25-200 watts, and in a variety of colours. Special shapes include candle bulbs, small and large spherical 'golf ball' bulbs, which look good in modern fittings, large spheres (again for fittings specially designed for their use), architectural strip lights (also sometimes called linear bulbs), for use as concealed lighting under shelves and kitchen wall units, and standard strip lights (slightly bigger than architectural strip lights and harder to conceal).

Certain spotlights are also powered by tungsten. PAR bulbs (Parabolic aluminized reflectors), for use outdoors because they are weatherproof, come as

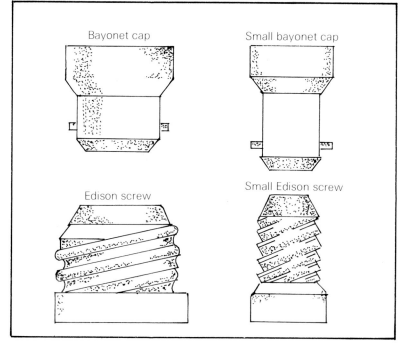

Bayonet cap

Small bayonet cap

Edison screw

Small Edison screw

Illustrated are four of the most common incandescent bulb bases although many more exist.

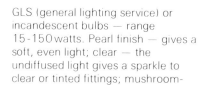

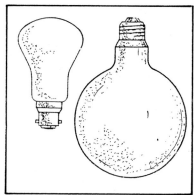

GLS (general lighting service) or incandescent bulbs — range 15-150 watts. Pearl finish — gives a soft, even light; clear — the undiffused light gives a sparkle to clear or tinted fittings; mushroom-

shaped — useful for small shades or where the bulb may be visible; large spherical bulbs — designed to be used in fittings where the bulb is visible.

Crown-silvered bulbs — range 40-100 watts. Designed to throw the light back onto a reflector to give a glare-free light.

spotlights, floodlights, wide-beam, narrow-beam and medium-beam bulbs. PAR 38 bulbs come as either spotlights or floodlights, in sizes from 75 to 150 watts. PAR 36 bulbs come in 25, 30 and 50 watt sizes. PAR 56, narrow, medium and wide-beam bulbs are all 300 watts.

ISL (internally silvered) and crown-silvered bulbs are designed either to focus the beam of the light (internally silvered), or throw it back against the fitting so that it does not dazzle anyone below (crown-silvered).

### Mains Voltage Tungsten-halogen Bulb

These bulbs have a longer life than conventional tungsten bulbs because evaporated matter from the filament is re-deposited on the filament itself (which has a quartz surround). This makes the bulb last twice as long as a conventional light bulb (but it does cost more to buy).

The light given by tungsten-halogen bulbs is whiter than the light given by conventional tungsten, so is particularly suitable for spotlights. Tungsten-halogen bulbs can be dimmed without the need for special fittings.

### Types of Tungsten-halogen Bulb

There are various types of spotlight bulbs designed for use on tracks. Linear tungsten-halogen lamps are used for powerful outdoor floodlighting, perfect if you want to light the whole of the front of your

PAR 38 (parabolic aluminized reflector) — range 75 - 150 watts. Powered by tungsten and made in strong glass, these bulbs are weather-proof and are therefore suitable for outdoor lighting.

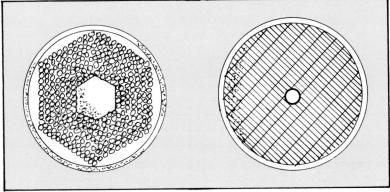

The designs on the front lenses of PAR 38s determine the type of beam. The corrugated design will produce a flood of light while the 'speckled' design will produce a narrow beam.

home. Narrow tungsten-halogen display bulbs are used for lighting displays, such as a shelf of glass or china.

## Low-voltage Tungsten-halogen Bulb

Low-voltage tungsten-halogen bulbs are probably the most exciting development in lighting since Edison made his first successful demonstration of the incandescent bulb. Low-voltage bulbs operate on either 12 or 24 volts, well below the mains rate of 240 volts. They are tiny — just a fraction of the size of a conventional tungsten-halogen bulb, so fittings can be discreetly recessed into the ceiling, allowing the flexibility of high-tech lighting without installing fittings out of character with the style of the room.

The light given off by these bulbs is crisp and white, particularly suitable for displaying paintings and sculpture. A softer effect can be achieved by choosing fittings with gold back reflectors.

As low-voltage bulbs run on a voltage much lower than that supplied by mains electricity, a transformer must be fitted to bring down the voltage to 12 or 24 volts. The transformer can be an integral part of the fitting, or can be remote from the bulbs. The advantage of the separate transformer is that the bulbs used with it are very small — ideal where discreet lighting is needed. One transformer can power several bulbs on one circuit, providing that they are all of the same voltage.

The transformer can be hidden away in a

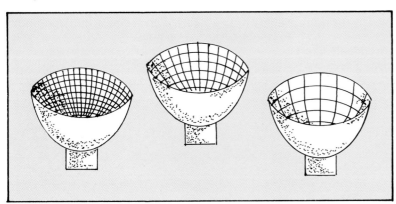

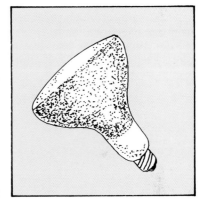

The inside of a multimirror bulb is surfaced with mirrored facets and the type of beam is dependent on the size and arrangement of these mirrors. The smaller and more numerous the facets, the narrower the beam will be, while those with large facets will produce a floodlight effect. They can be bought with a dichroic coating on the reflector which reflects visible light but allows infra-red light to pass backwards into the fitting behind the bulb.

ISL (internally silvered) bulbs are designed with an internal reflective coating which focuses the beam in a specific direction.

cupboard, the garage, or within the ceiling itself, providing that a trapdoor is made for access. Low-voltage transformers must be fitted by a qualified electrician.

### Types of Low-voltage Bulb

There are two basic types of low-voltage bulbs — with and without reflectors. Bulbs without reflectors will need some sort of reflector in the ceiling fitting, so that the light is directed downwards.

More useful are bulbs fitted with reflectors, sometimes known as multi-mirror. These come in beam angles from narrow to wide. Dichroic multi-mirror bulbs are designed so that the heat from the light is passed backwards into the fitting. This makes them suitable for use in a low-ceiling, or for lighting a delicate subject which could be harmed by the heat from a conventional bulb.

Low-voltage lights can also be directional, like tiny eyeballs fitted onto a jointed arm. These are useful for lighting collections and displays.

### Fluorescent Lighting

Fluorescents radiate a clear, white light. Electrons pass down the light tube and react with the phosphor coating to produce a fluorescent glow. The bulbs are long-lasting and energy efficient — and come in many different shapes and sizes. The major drawback, even though 'daylight corrected' fluorescents have been introduced, is that the light is harsh and unflattering, limiting domestic use.

### Types of Fluorescent Bulb

As well as the conventional tube light, which used to be favoured for kitchens, fluorescents come as mini tubes, for use under kitchen wall units and in a variety of task lights. These mini strips do not come in colour corrected versions.

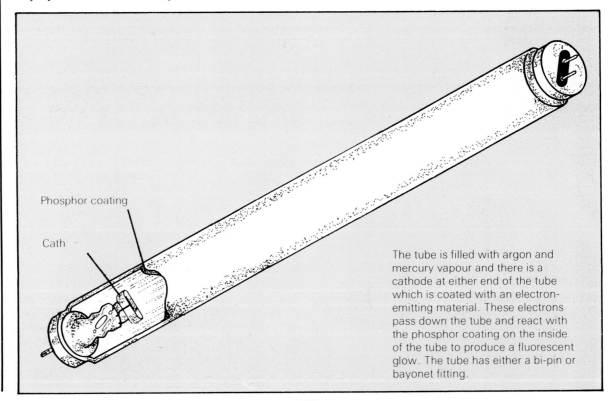

Phosphor coating

Cath

The tube is filled with argon and mercury vapour and there is a cathode at either end of the tube which is coated with an electron-emitting material. These electrons pass down the tube and react with the phosphor coating on the inside of the tube to produce a fluorescent glow. The tube has either a bi-pin or bayonet fitting.

## Metal-halide Bulb

Like fluorescents, metal-halide bulbs work on a gas discharge process. They were developed for industrial use and give a bluish light — limiting their possibilities in the home. Weatherproof metal-halides are good for lighting trees and other greenery — the bulb brings out the colour.

## Controls

However good your selection of fittings, no lighting system can work well without flexible controls. The more controls there are within the system, the better it will be. Imagine the possibilities of being able to dim general lighting separately from task lighting, or being able to dim some downlighters, leaving others bright. Modern dimmer switches make all of these interesting possibilities a reality — providing the system is properly designed and there are sufficient controls to give the effects you want.

Replacing a conventional light switch with a dimmer is one of the quickest ways to add flexibility and interest to lighting. Overhead or wall lights can be dimmed to provide background light, with plug-in lamps giving warm pools of accent.

An effective control system can only be achieved by having separately switched circuits for each set of light sources. This may seem expensive and unnecessary, but it is the only way to achieve true flexibility. In an average room, you would need dimmers for general downlighting, separate dimmers for display lighting (such as an eyeball spot directed to frame a picture with light) and for a pendant fitting such as a chandelier, separate again for wall lights or uplighters, with normal on/off switching for table lamps.

Remember, when working out the controls you need, that not all sources of light can be dimmed. Fluorescent lighting can only be dimmed by the use of special wiring. Controls themselves have come a

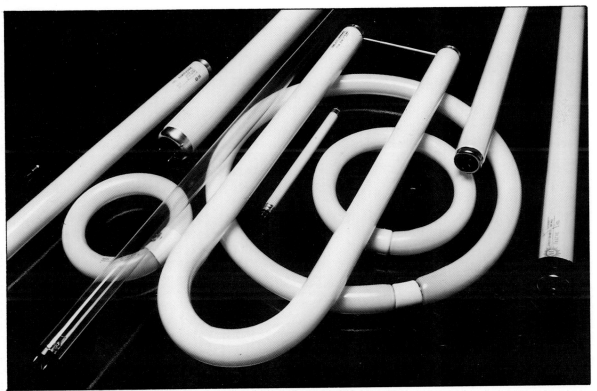

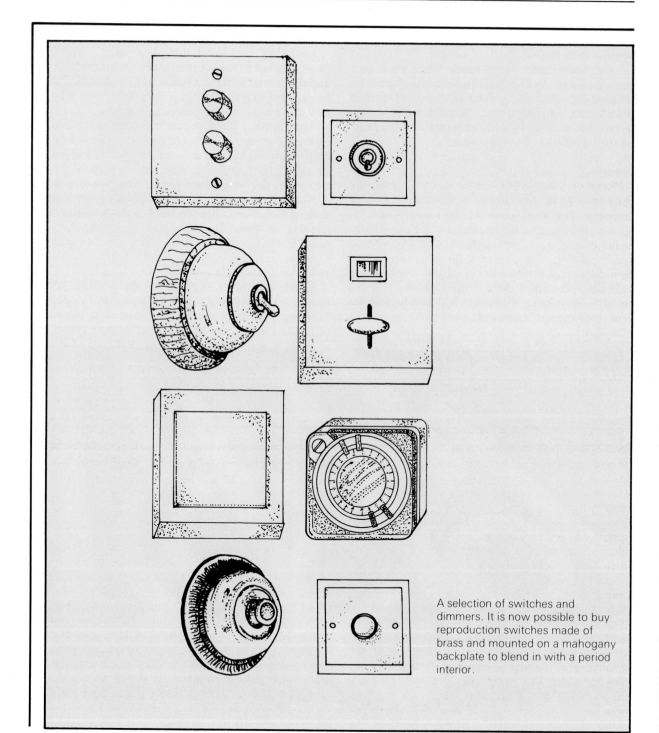

A selection of switches and dimmers. It is now possible to buy reproduction switches made of brass and mounted on a mahogany backplate to blend in with a period interior.

long way from the basic light switch. Dimmers are commonplace now, cheap and easy to install, and come in various designs and finishes, so the fitting need not clash with the style of the room.

With rotary dimmers the light comes on when the knob is turned clockwise and increases as the control is advanced. The drawback to this sort of dimmer is that it cannot be used in conjunction with another type of switching in the same room.

The on/off push type of switch operates the light when the knob is pushed down. Brightness is increased as the knob is turned. This sort of dimmer can be used for two-way switching, with dimming available on one switch only. When the light is switched off at the other end, the level of dimness remains set at the last selection.

On the slider type of dimmer, a rocker switch turns the light on while a second rocker controls the light level. The light can be switched off at any level.

In the case of multiple dimmers there are usually four rotary controls on one switch plate to control lights in sets of two. Using this sort of control, you could, for instance, light one area of a room, leaving the rest dark, or use bright light to display a picture or piece of sculpture, with other ceiling fittings dimmed.

Sophisticated electronic dimmers allow individual control of each light by means of a hand-held infra red remote controller. Another new development is the introduction of photo-electric cells into domestic lighting. These are used in bedrooms to light the room gradually — just as if dawn was breaking. These sophisticated fittings are, needless to say, expensive and not really worthwhile for domestic use unless you have a large, particularly splendid room which calls for the flexibility of individual controls.

## Choosing the Right Controls

Choosing controls is not simply a matter of selecting some you like the look of and having them installed. The rating of the control must match or exceed the rating of the fittings it will operate. If, for instance, you wanted a dimmer to control four 100 watt bulbs, the switch would need to have a rating of 400 watts or more. It is particularly important to check this if you are replacing conventional switches with dimmers without the help of a fully qualified electrician.

If you want to use a dimmer with low-voltage lighting, it must be one which has been adapted for this sort of fitting. Visit a specialist electrical shop where advice is available.

Where there are several fittings (such as six or more recessed downlighters), it is worth having a separate electronic dimming system installed to get the maximum possible effect from the lights. This sort of system allows you to set changes of light over a period of several seconds, so that the light dims or brightens gradually. It is also possible with this sort of system to have some of the lights dim and others bright.

## Fitting a Dimmer

Before buying a dimmer switch, take the cover off the existing light switch (turn the power off at the mains first). Make a note of how the switch is wired and measure the faceplate before you buy a dimmer. It is a good idea to take a diagram with you to the shop.

To fit the dimmer, switch off the power at the mains and remove the faceplate of the old switch, disconnecting all but the earth wire. Attach the wires to the faceplate of the dimmer. The connection points will be marked live/neutral. In lighting circuits, red/brown is live, neutral is black/blue. The faceplate of the dimmer can now be screwed into position and the power switched back on to test the switch. A conventional light switch can be fitted in the same way.

## Home Security

If you are often away from home, or out in the evenings, it is worth incorporating some security controls into lighting. Security controls come in the form of either bulb holders for use with table lamps or ceiling pendants or as switches. Bulb holder security fittings are fitted with a light sensitive cell which will switch the light on as soon as darkness falls, off again when it is daylight, or on and off at intervals, giving the impression that there is someone in the house. Light sensitive wall switches work in the same way. Timer switches can be plugged into wall sockets and timed to switch the television, radio or a lamp on and off at set times.

## CHAPTER 7

# SHADES TO MAKE

Although there is an enormous choice of lamps and shades in both chain stores and specialist lighting shops, the chance to decorate a room with a design of your own, adding your own touch of individuality, is always a welcome one. Moreover sometimes it is absolutely impossible to find a shade in a colour or fabric you want. Making your own shades is easy. All that is needed is a frame, fabric or paper to cover it and, if making a lamp, a suitable object for the base, a switched lamp holder and some cable.

Shades can be as simple or as complicated as you like. Even the most ham-fisted of us can manage a basic handkerchief shade, while those good at handiwork can embark upon more ambitious tailored and pleated designs.

**Lamp bases**

Almost any bottle, jar or vase can be used as a lamp base. All tall or lightweight containers must be given ballast with a little sand or gravel, otherwise the lamp will fall over once the shade and bulb are fitted. If the vase, jar or bottle is made from glass, obviously sand or gravel will not look attractive. However the problem can be simply overcome by filling the container with pretty stones (collect them from the beach); coloured gravel (from pet shops and aquarists); Christmas tree baubles in plain gold, silver, red or blue for festive sparkle; pine cones, left plain or sprayed gold or silver (put a few small stones in the bottom of the container to add weight — the pine cones will hide them); pot pourri (again mixed with a few stones), or glass marbles.

Tall, narrow-necked vases and bottles make ideal bases as a lampholder with adjustable flanges can be wedged into the neck. If the opening is wide, cut a piece of cork 5 cm (2 in) thick to fit snugly into the neck. You will then need to make a hole in the middle of the cork for the lampholder.

It is easiest to use the type of lampholder where the flex comes from the side rather than through the bottom. This looks a little untidy, but there are sound practical reasons for choosing this sort of fitting. On commercially-made lamps, the cable exits via a hole in either the base of the lamp or the side. Although it is possible to drill a hole in the base of most glass or ceramic containers, what you cannot do is make a notch in the side of the base so as to prevent the cable unbalancing the lamp. Drilling an exit hole in the side of the container is an operation fraught with hazard, so the dangling cable is the only practical option.

## Simple Shades

All lampshades are supported by a frame and these come in all shapes and sizes, from simple drums and coolie cones to elaborate six or eight-sided designs for tailored shades. Frames are made from either plain, painted or fabric-covered metal. However, if the frame is bare metal it is wise to paint it first to stop it rusting. A quick-drying cellulose paint of the type used for re-touching car bodywork is ideal. The next stage in preparing the frame is to bind it tightly with narrow cotton tape. It is not always essential to bind the struts as this can cause ridges which will show through the finished shade, but the top and bottom rings must be bound as this forms the foundation on to which the shade is fixed. It is important to bind the tape very tightly otherwise the finished shade will sag and twist. To do this, dab the end of the tape with a suitable glue and stick it to the lower edge of the frame. Keeping the tape at an acute angle, bind the tape tightly around both rings, and the struts if necessary, securing the other end firmly with glue.

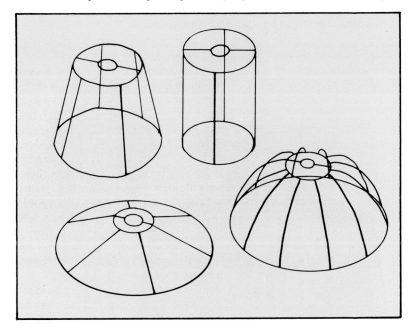

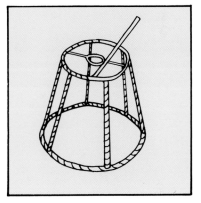

To bind the frame start with the top ring. Cut a piece of tape equal to twice the length of the circumference and glue it to the frame at the top of a strut at an angle. Begin binding the frame tightly, keeping the tape at an acute angle. The fabric of the shade will be stitched to this binding so it is important to keep the tape as tight as possible to avoid the finished shade sagging. Secure the other end with glue and trim any excess. Repeat with the bottom ring. Bind each strut in the same way.

All lampshades are supported by a frame. Frames come in all shapes and sizes, from simple drums and coolie cones to elaborate six or eight-sided designs for tailored shades. Frames are made from either plain, painted or fabric covered metal. Plain metal frames rust, so wrap them with thin fabric tape. This will also give a firm foundation to which the fabric of the shade can be pinned and stitched.

### The No-sew Shade

Handkerchief shades are blissfully simple to make. Drape a piece of fabric, a scarf or a large handkerchief over the frame of your choice. Cotton lace handkerchief shades look good in a room furnished with country antiques. The cotton lace can be left white or cream or dyed to the colour of your choice. Avoid using nylon lace, as it discolours. Alternatively two or three chiffon scarves, in complementary or contrasting colours, can look very effective. For safety's sake, cut a hole in the middle so that the heat from the bulb can escape and catch-stitch the edges of the hole to the frame to keep the shade in place.

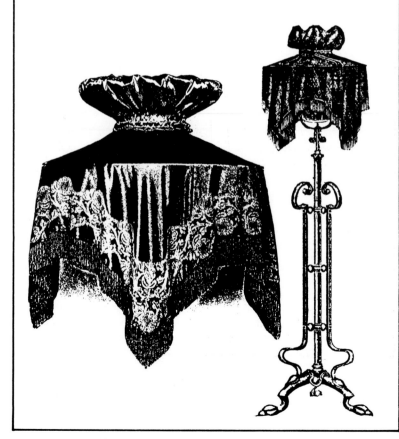

## Paper Shades

Strong drawing paper (sold in sheets by art shops) can be used to make both plain and pleated shades. Paper gives great scope for decorative ideas as it can be painted or stencilled (do this before the shade is made). Sponging, stippling, marbling and other paint effects work well, but use a water based paint. Alternatively, they can be made from remnants of wall paper to match the room. To stencil, use a stencil crayon kit (available from department stores). The stencil should ideally be kept to a small, simple design, such as a border of leaves or flowers, as big designs tend not to work well and can appear overpowering when the lamp is lit.

The simplest form of paper shade is made using a drum-shaped frame. Coolie-shaped shades are very fashionable and are quite straightforward to make once the pattern has been made. Pleated shades, popular in Victorian times are currently enjoying a revival and can be made easily following the instructions below.

The projects in this chapter will bring a touch of individuality and enable you to stamp your own personality on your home without breaking the bank. With the careful choice of materials, colours and patterns these shades can be made to suit any sort of decor, whether period, country or ultra-modern in style.

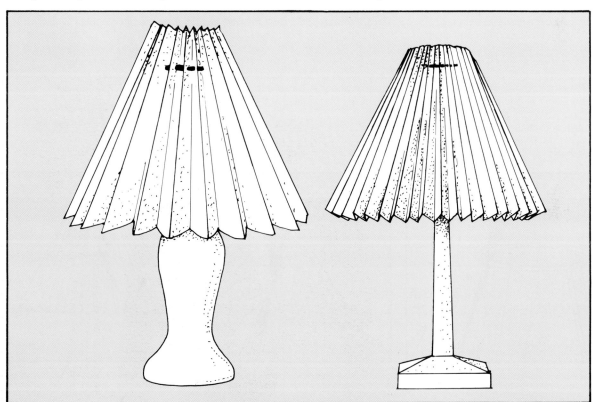

Pleated shades are currently enjoying a fashionable revival. They can be made from wrapping paper, marbled paper or a remnant from the wallpaper in the room. Do not use paper that is too thick or the light will not shine through.

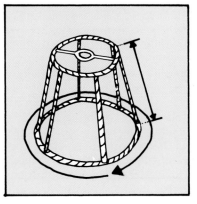

Using a cone-shaped frame that has already been covered with tape, measure the circumference of the bottom of the frame and double the measurement. Add 1 cm (⅜in) extra for gluing the shade together. Measure from top to bottom and add 5 cm (2 in) to the measurement. If you wish to cut a zig-zag edge make sure that the lower or upper ring of the frame will not be exposed.

Carefully fold the paper into even, narrow pleats, concertina fashion. Ideally the pleats should be between 2-3 cm (¾-1¼in). Press each fold down firmly with your thumbnail. Pleating can be practised on a spare piece of paper to be sure that the size of the folds will give the effect desired.

Use a hole punch to make a hole in the centre of each pleat 2.5 cm (1 in) from the top. Alternatively, pierce the hole with a needle and then with a knitting needle.

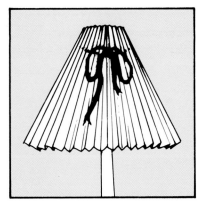

Just above the holes for the ribbon punch a half hole in the edge of the pleats to fix the shade to the frame. Alternatively, cut small notches.

If a zig-zag effect is desired cut each pleat separately otherwise the result will be uneven. Glue the side edge to the 1 cm (⅜in) allowance and leave to dry. Thread thin cord or narrow ribbon through the holes.

Place the paper shade onto the frame and position the notches over the frame. Tighten the ribbon or cord until it fits well and tie the end in a knot or a bow. The ribbon or cord can be catch-stitched to the frame on the inside.

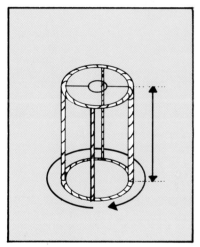

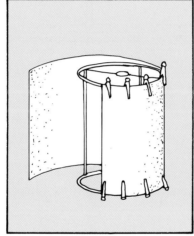

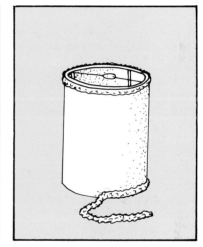

To make a paper shade, you will need a drum shaped frame, the rings of which have already been covered with tape. Measure around the frame and add ½in. Measure from top to bottom. Cut the paper to these measurements.

Carefully spread glue down one narrow edge of the paper and along both long edges. Roll carefully around the frame, securing the paper to the top and bottom with large paper clips or clothes pegs. Stick the two narrow edges together.

When the glue is dry, stitch the paper to the top and bottom struts of the shade. Cover the stitching by sticking lampshade braid (available from department stores) around the top and bottom edges.

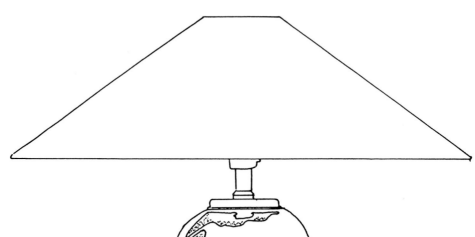

If you want to make a coolie-shaped shade, the principals are the same as for the drum-shaped, however as the rings, top and bottom, are a different size it will be necessary to cut a pattern.

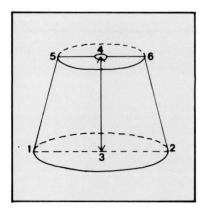

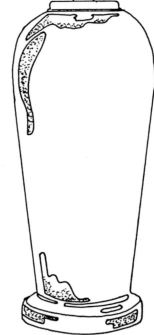

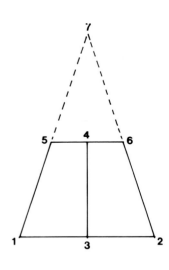

Measure the frame, taking note of the height of the struts, the circumference of the top and bottom rings and the diameter of the top and bottom ring.

In the bottom left hand corner of a large sheet of graph paper draw a horizontal line (1-2) equal to the measurement of the diameter of the bottom ring.

Find the centre of the line (3) and draw a line at right angles to the height of the shade (4)
Draw another line equal to the diameter of the top ring using point 4 as the centre. Join points 1-5 and 2-6 together and extend these lines until they meet at point 7.

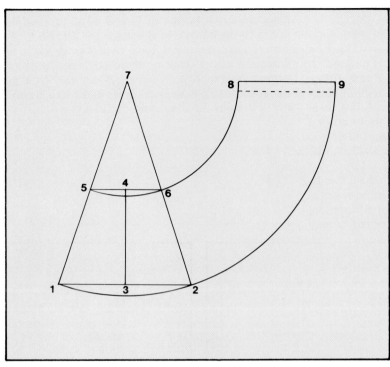

Cut around the lines 1 - 5 - 8 - 9 and this gives the finished paper pattern. Check it for fit against the frame. Use the pattern to cut out the stiffened fabric or paper of your choice and proceed as for the drum-shaped shade.

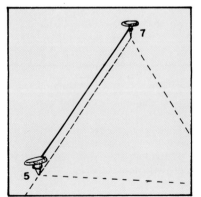

To draw the arc 5 - 8, stretch a piece of string tied to two drawing pins along the line 5 - 7.

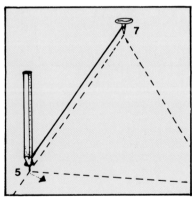

Remove the pin at point 5 and insert the point of a pencil. Keeping the pencil upright draw an arc equal to the circumference of the top ring of the shade.

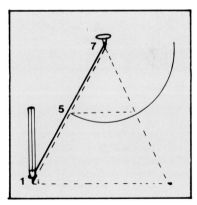

To draw the arc 1 - 9, stretch a piece of string between two pins along the line 7 - 1 and proceed as before, drawing an arc equal to the circumference of the bottom ring. Extend the two arcs by 2 cm (½in) to allow for an overlap when gluing the shade and join up points 8 - 9.

# SHADES TO MAKE

### Simple Gathered Shade

Although this shade involves some sewing, it is not necessary to be an expert. However, you will need a sewing machine to make a neat seam. The frame is dome-shaped and the cover is semi-fitted, fitting tightly at the bottom, but gathering in to fit the much narrower top. It is simple to make, with just three seams — one to join the fabric together to make a tube and a hem, top and bottom, to take the elastic. An added advantage with this type of shade is that the cover can be removed for washing.

There are a variety of ways that the shade can be trimmed depending on the look you wish to achieve. A frill, single or double, can be added either using matching fabric or a complementary or contrasting plain colour. A border of lace or beading could be added to the bottom of the shade for a 1930s look. An effective treatment for a bedroom shade is to make the cover from broderie anglaise, finishing with a double frill. Narrow ribbon can then be threaded through the eyelet holes in the lace around the bottom of the shade and tied in a bow.

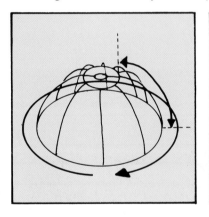
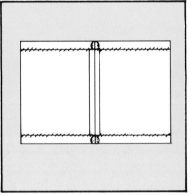
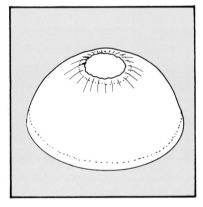

Although this shade involves some sewing, you do not need to be an expert. However, you will need a sewing machine to make a neat seam. Using a dome-shaped frame which has already been bound with tape as shown on page 132, measure around the bottom and add 2.5 cm (1 in) for the seam. Measure from top to bottom and add 2.5 cm (1 in) for hems. Cut a piece of fabric to these measurements.

With right sides of the fabric together seam the fabric along the narrow ends. Turn over a 1 cm (½ in) hem at top and bottom. Catch-stitch in place, leaving an opening close to the side seam.

Thread lengths of elastic slightly shorter than the top and bottom measurement around the lampshade through these hems. Stitch the ends of the elastic together then close the seams. Turn the shade right side out and pull it over the frame. Even out the gathers.

## CHAPTER 8

Tracking down the real thing in light fittings, rather than opting for reproduction, is not as difficult or as expensive as it sounds. There are many specialists in antique lighting, with prices ranging from reasonable to high, depending on the age and style of the item. Street markets, jumble sales and junk shops are also good sources of light fittings. Scour the sales lists for local auctions — country house sales are particularly worthwhile as it is often possible to buy a job lot of fittings. Some will be useless, but most lots include brass and wooden switches, shades needing minor repair and interesting bases, all of which can add an original touch to your home.

When buying electrical fittings from sources such as jumble sales, markets and auctions, examine them carefully. Look out for signs of scorching around terminals — these can indicate that complete re-wiring is needed. Old pendant fittings will inevitably need to be re-wired to suit modern lighting installations. Most electricians can do this for a small charge. Check the wiring of chandeliers carefully — there are often breaks in the cabling leading up to each individual bulb. Again, re-wiring is possible, but will need to be carried out by a chandelier specialist. Chandelier specialists can also clean crystal and repair or replace missing pieces. If you buy a fitting and are in any doubt about safety, take it to an electrician.

Look at the condition of the body of the fitting.

Tarnished brass is easy to clean at home — buy a proprietary cleaning product and follow manufacturer's instructions. Badly damaged gilded fittings are more difficult to repair and may need expensive specialist care. Only buy these if you are willing to pay for this. Small pieces of missing gilding can usually be replaced by filling the area with wall filler, sanding it to shape, then painting it with antique gilding. Be sure to buy gilding described as suitable for aged work or you will have a bright gold patch.

Other things worth looking out for are large, decorative vases suitable for use as lamp bases (instructions for turning a vase into a lamp base appear on page 132), tins of the type used for storing tea or coffee in old-fashioned grocer's shops, again

suitable as bases, and interestingly shaped lampshades. It does not matter if the fabric is badly worn — it can be removed or replaced. Brass, glass, china or silver candlesticks are always worth having, even if the only time you use them is for dinner parties. Wooden candlesticks are attractive, and can be sponged, stippled, marbled or stencilled to suit decor and soft furnishings. Wide, shallow china and glass bowls are worth having too — fill them with water and flowers, and float night lights among them.

You might still be lucky enough to find a china, glass or brass oil lamp at a country sale — though you will probably have to compete with collectors for these. Lamps can be converted to electricity, but are really much nicer left in their original state.

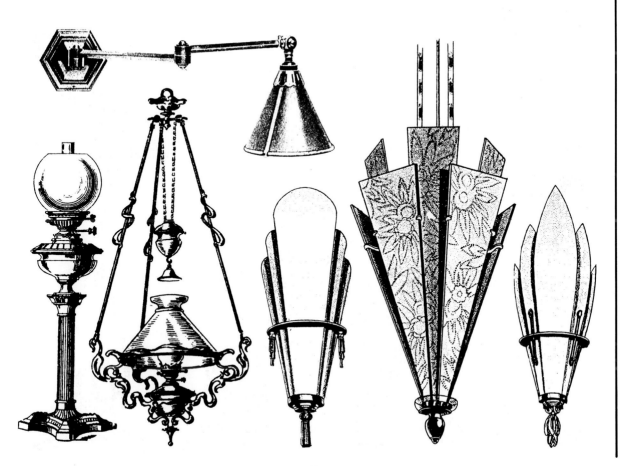

The companies and shops listed here all specialize in the supply of reproduction and antique light fittings. Many of them will supply by mail order.

Period fittings can often be found at auctions and country house sales. Before you have a fitting installed, the wiring must be checked. Several of the specialists listed here are able to restore and rewire antique fittings, or convert them to electricity.

Best & Lloyd Ltd
William St West
Smethwick
Warley
West Midlands B66 2NX
Suppliers of brass candle sconces in the style of Adam and Hepplewhite. Also large stock of Victorian pendant fittings.

The Birmingham Glass Studios Ltd
Unit 5, 102 Edward Road
Balsall Heath
Birmingham B11 3SA
Specialist in antique and reproduction coloured glass, including Tiffany-style shades.

R.J. Chelsom & Co Ltd
Squires Gate Industrial Estate
Blackpool
Lancashire FY4 3RN
A treasure trove of reproduction fittings covering a time span of around 200 years. Styles in stock include Victorian, period American, Adam, French, Georgian and Flemish. Catalogue and lists of stockists nationwide.

Mrs M.E. Crick Ltd
166 Kensington Church St
London W8 4BN
Specialist in eighteenth to twentieth century lighting. Large stock in crystal and ormolu.

T Crowther & Son Ltd
282 North End Road
London W8 7DU
Crowther's is one of the most famous antique shops in London, with enormous stocks of interior period detail, such as mouldings and cornices, and exterior sculpture and statuary. They also stock eighteenth-century light fittings and are well worth a visit.

Delomosne & Son Ltd
4 Campden Hill Road
London W8 7DU
Antique shop specializing in eighteenth and nineteenth-century English crystal chandeliers.

Dernier & Hamlyn Ltd
17 Lydden Road
London SW18 4LT
One of the most established lighting companies. They specialize in high-quality traditional fittings. Clients can commission their own designs, and a restoration service is offered.

David Fileman Antiques
Squirrels
Bayards
Horsham Road
Steyning
West Sussex BN4 3AA
Restoration of period fittings. Also stockist of antique candelabra, chandeliers and fittings ranging from Georgian to Art Deco.

Fritz Fryer Decorative Antique Lighting
12 Brook End Street
Ross-on-Wye
Herefordshire HR9 7EG
Antique lighting from Georgian to Art Deco. Specialist advice and fitting.

Jones (Lighting)
194 Westbourne Grove
London W11
Jones claim to have the largest selection of original light fittings in Europe. Worth a visit.

The Lamp Gallery
355 New Kings Road
London SW6 4RJ
The Lamp Gallery specializes in late-Victorian, Edwardian, Art Deco and Art Nouveau wall-lights, chandeliers and table lamps. Good advice and a full restoration service are offered to clients.

Lots Road Antique Galleries
71 Lots Road
London SW10 0RN
Lots Road is an auction house that holds regular sales of period lamps and fittings, as well as furniture and fine art sales.

Planet Shades Ltd
PO Box 118
Lampard Grove
London N16 8XB
Makers of silk and fabric lampshades to customer requirements. Also antique brass chandeliers, wall brackets, glass shades, wall pendants and other Victorian and Edwardian fittings.

R&S Robertson Ltd
Unit 13
36 Bankhead Drive
Sighthill Industrial Estate
Edinburgh EH11 4EQ
Makers of one-off designs to customer requirements and of a large range of period fittings.
Catalogue available.

W Sitch & Co Ltd
48 Berwick St
London W1 4JD
Specialist in nineteenth century chandeliers, wall brackets and floor lights. Also repair and restore, re-gild and bronze.

Sugg Lighting Ltd
Sussex Manor Business Park
Gatwick Road
Crawley
W. Sussex RH10 2GD
Established in 1807, Sugg Lighting is the original lighting company; they pioneered early gas street lamps. Today, they still make lamps, both outdoor and indoor, to the same Victorian designs and using traditional materials and techniques. They also still manufacture gas lamps, which are becoming popular again, will make one-off designs on commission and offer a full restoration service.

A & H Brass Ltd
201-203 Edgware Road
London W2

Ampersand
62 Park Road
London NW1 4SH

Anglian Lamps (Overseas) Ltd
45 Mill Road
Kettering
Northants

Anglepoise Lighting Ltd
Enfield Industrial Estate
Redditch B97 6DR

Architectural Antiques
Savoy Showroom
New Road
South Molton
Devon

Architectural Trading Company
1-2 Cosser Street
London SE1

Argon
17 Neal Street
London WC2

Artemide GB Ltd
17-19 Neal Street
London WC2H 9PU

Astrohome Ltd
47/49 Neal Street
Covent Garden
London WC2

Astbury Lighting Ltd
Elizabeth Mill
Worrall Street
Congleton
Cheshire CW12 1DT

Aurora Lighting Ltd
9 John Dalton Street
Manchester 2

Belgravia Arts Ltd
4 Ferrard Close
Ascot
Berks SL5 8LN

Best & Lloyd Ltd
William Street West
Smethwick
Warley
West Midlands

Bieffeplast
OMK Design Ltd
The Stephen Building
30 Stephen Street
London W1

Brillantleuchten
35-36 Floral Street
London WC2 9DJ

Peter Burian Associates
Hill View
Vale of Health
London NW3 1AN

Candlelight Products Ltd
3-4 Parkhouse Lane
Tinsley
Sheffield S9 1XA

Casa Fina
132 Notting Hill Gate
London W11

R.J. Chelsom & Co Ltd
Squires Gate Industrial Estate
Blackpool
Lancs FY4 3RN

Chinoiserie Ltd
11-15 Headfort Place
Belgrave Square
London SW1X 7DE

Ciel at Christopher Lawrence
281 Lillie Road
London SW6

Margery Clinton Ceramics
The Pottery
Newton Poryt
Haddington
East Lothian

Colourflair Furniture Ltd
29 Bruton Street
London W1

Concord Lighting Ltd
Concord House
241 City Road
London EC1V 1JD

The Copper Lamp Co Ltd
Unit D
Nutts Lane
Hinkley
Leics LE10 3EJ

Courtney Pope Lighting Ltd
Amhurst Park Works
Tottenham
London N15 6RB

Cresswell Shades Ltd
7 Green Drift
Royston
Herts SG8 5DD

John Cullen Lighting
1 Woodall Court
Smith Street
London SW3

N Davigni
117 Shepherd's Bush Road
London W6

Davniglass Handcraft
29 Abbots Close
Shenfield
Essex CM15 8LT

Dernier and Hamlyn Ltd
17 Lydden Road
London SW18 4LT

Design Carvill Ltd
12 Hunter Road
Wimbledon
London SW20 8NZ

Designers Guild
271/277 King's Road
London SW3 5EN

The Dining Room Shop
64 White Hart Lane
Barnes
London SW13

Doverlight Ltd
47 Ruddell Crescent
London NW3 1RR

Elizabeth Eaton
25a Basil Street
London SW3 1BB

Edison Halo Ltd
Eskdale Road
Uxbridge Industrial Estate
Uxbridge
Middlesex UB8 2RT

Eleusi per Illuminaire
Walter International
42 High Street
Daventry
Northants

Elit Lighting
279 Wimbledon Park Road
London SW19 6NW

Emess Lighting (UK) Ltd
6 Anderson Road
Roding Lane South
Woodford Green
Essex

End of Day Lighting Co
44 Parkway
London NW1

Nicholas Eugert Interior Design
2 Inch's Yard
Market Street
Newbury
Berks

Equinox Interiors Ltd
64-72 New Oxford Street
London WC1

Forma Ltd
Victor Mann & Co Ltd
Unit 3, Mitcham Industrial Estate
85 Streatham Road
Mitcham
Surrey

Mary Fox Linton Ltd
249 Fulham Road
London SW3 6HY

Franklite Ltd
1 Bridgeturn Avenue
Old Wolverton Road
Milton Keynes MK12 5QL

The Garden Lighting Co
352 York Road
London SW18 1SS

Thomas Goode & Co (London) Ltd
19 South Audley Street
London W1Y 6BN

Graham & Green Ltd
4 & 7 Elgin Crescent
London W11

Hammond Wholesale
7b Harriet Walk
London SW1X 9JQ

Norman Harrap & Son
238 Spring Bank
Hull HU3 1LU

Thomas Haywood & Son Ltd
33 Avery Hill Road
New Eltham
London SE9 2BW

Hitech (UK) Ltd
Tower House
Lea Valley Trading Estate
Edmonton
London N18 3HR

Hoffmeister Lighting Ltd
Units 3 & 4
Preston Road
Reading
Berks

Oswald Hollman Ltd
208 Kent House Road
Beckenham
Kent BR3 1JN

Homelight Exhibition Centre
(N. M. Lighting)
110 Goodmayes Road
Ilford
Essex IG3 9UZ

Homeworks Ltd
107a Pimlico Road
London SW1

David Hunt Lighting Ltd
Tilemans Lane
Shipston-on-Stour
Warwicks CV36 4HP

Huntingdon Enterprise Ltd
Church Street
Stow-on-the-Wold
Glos GL4 1BB

Illumin
82 Bond Street
Macclesfield
Cheshire SK11 6QS

Inside Art
1-3 Petersfield Road
Bordon
Hants

Interbrass Ltd
404 The Highway
London E14 8DZ

Jones
194 Westbourne Grove
London W11

Kawala's Stained Glass Studio
54 Metropolitan Workshop
Enfield Road
London N1 5AZ

The Lamp Gallery
355 New King's Road
London SW6 4RJ

The Last Detail
341 Kings Road
London SW3

Christopher Lawrence Textiles &
Lighting Ltd
281 Lillie Road
London SW6 7LN

Lead & Light
15 Camden Lock
Commercial Place
London NW1 8AF

Le Dauphin
Malmesbury
Wilts SN16 9JX

Leisure Plan Sales
28 Windmill
Bishop's Stortford
Herts CM23 2NG

Freda Lewis Chandeliers
73 Elgin Crescent
London W11 2JE

Lewylite
The Lamp Works
201 Hornsey Road
London N7 6RA

Libra Designs Art Deco
Unit 45
Alfie's Antique Market
Church Street
London NW8

The Lighting Workshop
35-36 Floral Street
Covent Garden
London WC2E 9DJ

Lita
190 City Road
London EC1V 2QR

Lots Road Antique Galleries
71 Lots Road
London SW10 0RN

Martin Lighting Ltd
Hanworth Trading Estate
Hampton Road West
Feltham
Middlesex TW13 6DR

Miranda Contracts Ltd
6a Bessborough Place
London SW1V 3SH

Arnold Monrose Ltd
47-48 Berners Street
London W1P 3AD

Mr Light
275 Fulham Road
London SW10

279 King's Road
London SW3

307 Brompton Road
London SW3

Maxine Naylor
177 Waller Road
London SE14

Nice Irma's Ltd (Fabrication)
46 Googe Street
London W1P 1FJ

Orgatech Ltd
42 Gorst Road
London NW10 6LD

Caroline Petre
54 Westcroft Square
London W6 0TA

Pipe Dreams Ltd
103 Regent's Park Road
London NW1 8UR

Planet Shades Ltd
PO Box 118
28 Lampard Grove
London N16 6XB

Poole Lighting
Cabot Lane
Creekmoor
Poole
Dorset BH17 7BY

The Pot Light Company
45 Oxford Gardens
Chiswick
London W4 3BN

Prima Lighting Ltd
151 Deans Lane
Edgware
Middlesex HA8 9NY

R&S Robertson Ltd
44 Queen Street
Edinburgh EH2 3NL

Unit 316
Business Design Centre
Upper Street
London N1 0QH

The R. B. C. Trading Company Ltd
Cosgrove Hall
Cosgrove
Milton Keynes MK19 7JB

Carlos Remes Lighting Co
10 New Quebec Street
London W1H 7DD

RoChamp
Montpellier Retreat
off Suffolk Road
Cheltenham
Glos GL50 2XG

Roger of London
344 Richmond Road
East Twickenham
Middx

Adrian Sankey
Rydal Road
Ambleside
Cumbria

SC Products
73 Westbourne Park Road
London W2 5QH

Roy Smith & Son
63 Totteridge Lane
Whetstone
London N20

Smithbrook Ltd
Smithbrook
Cranleigh
Surrey

Stuart Interiors
Barrington Court
Barrington
Ilminster
Somerset TA19 0NQ

The Studio
117 Old Brompton Road
London SW7 3RN

Sugg Lighting Ltd
Sussex Manor Business Park
Gatwick Road
Crawley
W. Sussex RH10 2GD

Tag Design Partnership
39-41 North Road
London N7 9DP

Temple Lighting
Stockwell House
1 Stockwell Lane
Wavendon
Milton Keynes MK17 8LS

Tempus Stet Ltd
Trinity Business Centre
305/309 Rotherhithe Street
London SE16 1EY

Thousand and One Lamps Ltd
4 Barmeston Road
London SE6 3BN

Sally Townsend (WRAPPA)
14 Upland Road
London SE22 9EE

Waterford-Aynsley Ltd
Portland Works
Longton
Stoke-on-Trent
Staffs ST3 1HS

Oscar Woollens — Interiors International
421 Finchley Road
London NW3 6HL

Christopher Wray's Lighting Emporium
600 King's Road
London SW6 2DX

DESIGNERS

At Home
44 Newnham Road
Cambridge CB3 9EY

Cohen & Pearce Period Interiors
West Lavington Manor
West Lavington
Devizes
Wiltshire SN10 4LA

Mister Smith Interiors
1-3 The Parade
Croft Road
Crowborough
East Sussex TN6 1DR

Sue Stowell Fabrics and Wallpapers
813 Fulham Road
London SW6

Mark Wilkinson Furniture Ltd
126 Holland Park Avenue
London W11

**FRANCE**

L'Abat Jour Style
27 Ruelle Labbe
Vert en Drouais
28500 Vernouillet

Atelier 89
Les Bourderons
89116 Sepeaux

Charles
27 Rue de Paris
93100 Montreuil

La Chaumière
4 Rue Père de Foucauld
58000 Nevers

Delisle
4 Rue de Parc Royal
75003 Paris

Denoyelle et Fils
68 Rue des Rondeaux
75020 Paris

Paul Dutard
71 Rue Charlot
75003 Paris

P. Fourcoux
24 Passage Gustave Lepeu
75011 Paris

Feuka
156 Bld de Plombières
13014 Marseille

Lucien Gau
2 Rue de la Roquette
75011 Paris

P Gaudard
Morbier
39400 Morex

KBM
13 Rue de L'Industrie
68260 Kingersheim

Leconte
Rue Menneret
Tavers — BP9
45190 Beaugency

Max Leverrier
30 Rue Deparcieux
75014 Paris

Lita
5 Allée Verte
41600 Lamotte Beuvron

La Luciole
21 Pontgouin
28190 Courville

Lum
71 Rue de la Plaine
75020 Paris

Mathieu Luminaire FD
143 Avenue des Chutes Lavie
13013 Marseille

Les Lampes Annick Naudy
Château D'Asnières
Cizay la Madeleine
49700 Doue la Fontaine

Lux Abat Jour
ZI de la Voivre
88000 Epinal

Megalit
Zone Industrielle du Breuil
BP 55
18400 Saint Florent sur Cher

Petitot
10 Rue Verbois
75003 Paris

M Pradier et Fils
La Bregère
Boulazac
24000 Périgueux

Lanternes Pradier
RN 20
36250 Saint Maur

Redalum France
Zac la Gloriette
Chatte
38160 Saint Marcellin

Relux
ZI Route Departmentale 28#Reyrieux
01600 Trevoux

Rous
Avenue Voltaire
82000 Montauban

Terras
24 Rue Saint Gervais
69008 Lyon

Veronese
184 Bd Haussmann
75008 Paris

Wattohm
18/26 Rue Goubet
75940 Paris

## GERMANY

Aro-Leuchten GmbH
POB 1140
D-43280 Borken

Bankamp-Leuchten GmbH
POB 1209
D-5760 Arnsberg 1
Neheim Hüsten

Brendel Leuchtengesellschaft GmbH &
Co KG
Mecklenburgische Str 28-30
D-1000 Berlin 33

Brumberg Leuchten GmbH
POB 1120
D-5768 Sundern-Westenfeld

Compass Lichttechnik GmbH
POB 11 17
D-5768 Sundern
Westenfeld

ERCO Leuchten GmbH
POB 2460
D-5880 Lüdenscheid Fabrik
Brockhauser Weg 80-82

Aloys Fischer GmbH
Beleuchtungskörperfabrik
POB 1209
D-5768 Sundern 1

Goldkant-Leuchten
Fritz Wauer GmbH & Co KG
POB 22 03 80
D-5600 Wuppertal 22

Hillebrand Leuchten
Egon Hillebrand GmbH & Co
POB 17 60
D-5760 Arnsberg 1
Neheim

Holtkötter GmbH
FH-Leuchten
Käpenweg 13-17
D-14780 Lippstadt
Bad Waldliesborn

Walter Hustadt GmbH & Co KG
POB 1780
D-5760 Arnsberg 1
Kurt Jarmuth GmbH & Co
POB 1149
D-4770 Soest

Erich Krieg GmbH & Co
Ostenschlahstr 36
D-5870 Hemer

Licht GmbH & Co KG
POB 1740
D-6370
Oberusel 1

Müller & Zimmer GmbH & Co
Hasenbergstr 31/1
D-7000 Stuttgart 1

Ernst Palme GmbH & Co KG
POB 31 20
D-3538 Marsberg 3 (Westheim)

Rapid Leuchten GmbH
POB 1128
D-7301
Deizisau

Robers Leuchten GmbH & Co KG
Weseker Weg 36
D-4286 Südlohn 2

Schröder & Co GmbH
Beleuchtungskörperfabrik
In der Sohle 36
D-5760 Arnsberg 1
Neheim-Hüsten

Staff GmbH & Co KG
Leuchtenwerk Lemgo
POB 760
D-4920 Lemgo 1

Schulz & Adam GmbH
Wohnraumleuchten
Sohnreystr 8
D-3471 Lauenförde/Weser

Teka-Leuchten
Theodor Krägeloh & Comp
POB 2129 U 2130
D-5885 Schalksmühle 2

Simmermann & Co GmbH
Wohnraumleuchten-Fabrik
POB 11 20
D-6958 Limbach

Tempe-Lampen GmbH
POB 107
D-4930 Detmold

Weseler Leuchten GmbH & Co KG
Mindener Str 183
D-4900 Herford

E. G. Zimmermann GmbH
POB 2351
D-6450 Hanau

**ITALY**
Alva Line SAS
Via Bassa Dei Sassi 28
40100 Bologna

Anselmo & Valenti SNC
Via G Puccini 253
50041 Calenzano FI

AR FAR Luce Studio
Via Savona 67/A
20144 Milano

Arte Medicea SAS
Via Prov. Traversa Limitese 100/A/B
50053 Spichio — Vinci FI

Artemide SPA
Via Brugheira
20010 Pregnana Milanese MI

Basilux SRL
Via Erizzo 129
31049 Valdobbiadene TV

Bellagamba International SRL
Via Visconti di Modrone 27
20122 Milano

Bernardi Sergio
Via B. Verro 17
20141 Milano

Biagini Giorgio
Stradone di Rovezzano 30
50136 Firenze

C.I.L. Italia SRL
Via P. Santacroce 128
00167 Roma

Casey Fantin
Via G.M. Cecchi 23/A
50126 Firenze

Colorada Illuminazione SRL
Via Montello 15
35010 Trebaseleghe PD

Cos. Mo
Via del Forte Trionfale 6
00136 Roma

Elle Quattro SNC
Via R. Busoni 9/11/13 Z.I.
50053 Empoli FI

Fiam Elettronica
Via Regio Parco 32
10036 Settimo Torinese TO

Foscarini SPA
F. TE Manin 1
30121 Murano VE

Il Fanale SNC
Via Postumia Centro 14
31048 S. Biagio di Callalta TV

Lamp-Art
Via Dante 21
22070 Rovello Porro CO

Leucos SRL
Via Treviso 77
30037 Scorze VE

Linea Lux SRL
Via Giarizzo 3
19020 Ceparana SP

Longoboard SNC
Strada del Casalino 1
37127 Verona VR

Luceplan Contract SRL
Via Bellinzona 48
20155 Milano

Lumina Italia SRL
Via Donatori del Sangue
20010 Arluno MI

Luxgianka International SPA
Via Nuova Valassina 356
20035 Lissone MI

Minluce SNC
Via Flavio Gioia 20
37135 Verona

Molin Illuminazione SNC
Via Pascoli 20/A
30020 Quarto D'Altino VE

Nuova Irilux SRL
Via S. Gimignano 88
53036 Poggibonsi SI

Nuova Traviganti
Via Novi 7
20144 Milano

O. M. A. SRL
Via Tunisi 26
35135 Padova

Piu' Luce SRL
Via Bardella 8
36100 Vicenza

Quattrifolio SPA
Via Vigevano 33
20144 Milano

Sicme Illuminazione SRL
Via Triumplina 25/U
25127 Brescia

Star Glas SNC
Via del Vetro 29
30020 Marcon VE

Zonca SPA
Via Lomellina 145
27058 Voghera PV

**THE NETHERLANDS**

Artlite
Postbus 709
9200 AS Drachten

W. van Doorn en Zonen
Postbus 5
4100 AA Culemborg

Philips Lighting B.V.
Building EC2
5600 MD Eindhoven

Gebr. Berkes v.o.f.
Postbus 13
5130 AA Alphen

Corodox B.V.
Postbus 10
2040 AA Zandvoort

Eurolicht Lichtarchitectuur B.V.
Postbus 5070
1410 AB Nasarden

Metaalwarenfabriek den Haan Rotterdam
B.V.
Wijnhaven 81
3011 WK Rotterdam

Hogro B.V.
Postbus 265
5140 AG Waalwijk

Schreder B.V.
Postbus 105
3960 BC Wijk bij Duurstede

Tuynman B.V.
Postbus 96
1300 AB Almere

**SPAIN**

Acapri, S.A.
Julián Camarillo 18
Madrid 17

Aguado Martinez, Francisco
Carcagente 3
Valencia 7

Arteferro
Avenida Sánchez Pizjuán 63
Sevilla

Iberiten, S.A.
Saleta 5 y 7
Barcelona 28

Industrias Cabrera, S.A.
Violante de Hungria 69
Barcelona 28

Industrias F. G. — Francisco Garcia
Garcia
Tuberiá 4
Alicante

Industrias Luz, S.A.
Villar 81
Barcelona 26

Lamparas Joyfran-Adolfo Jesus Garcia
Garcia
Plaza Salvador Allende 8
Valencia 19

Lamparas Luyfe-Felipe del Baño Palazón
Velásquez 24 bajo
Valencia 8

Lamparas Ramagosa, S.A.
Traversa de Gracia 83
Barcelona 6

Lampisteria Sánchez
Camino del Baden 85
Murcia

Lumen
Monasterio de Nuestra Señora de
Valvanera 4
Zaragoza 2

Martin Caballero, Manuel
Poligono Navisa c/A 1
Sevilla 6

Moreno Paterna, José A.
Polgono Industrial El Pino
Parcelo 1, nave 13
Sevilla 16

Navarro Illuminacion, S.A.
Aurreoechea 1
Bilbao 6

Peréz Arroyo, Fernando ''J.P.''
Pico Cejo 22
Madrid 18

Sorianpo Sanahuja, Manuel
Cura Femenia 20
Valencia 6

Talleres Cerrarte
Los Guindos 5
(Barrio La Hoya)
San Sebastian de Los Reyes

Vialso, S. L.
Conde Torrefiel 9
Olleria (Valencia)

Viuda de Manuel Holguin
Carlos Daban 18
Madrid 19

Ace Lamps & Tubes Pty Ltd
6 Hopkins Street
Greensborough
Melbourne

Adam Lighting
85 Frenchmans Road
Randwick
New South Wales

Artcraft Metal Industries Pty Ltd
6 Monahan Avenue
Banksia
New South Wales 2216

Artemide Pty Ltd
69 Edward
Pyrmont
Sydney

Australian Lamp Importers & Distributors
Pty Ltd
662 Whitehorse Road
Mitcham
Melbourne

Attractive Lighting
50G Amy Street
Regents Park
New South Wales

Australian Lighting
Arndale Shopping Centre
Mt Dandenong Road
Victoria
(and branches)

Beam Light Gardens
1 Durkin Point
Parkhurst
Sydney

Brass Discovery
Shop 3
672 Glenferrie Road
Hawthorn
Victoria

The Brass Lamp
258 Milperra Road
Milperra
Sydney

Brodie R J Lighting Co
24 Belmore Road
Punchbowl
New South Wales

Cascade Lighting
Lower Mall
Chadstone Shopping Centre
Victoria

Chatswood Furniture & Lighting
216 Victoria Avenue
Chatswood
Sydney

Chadstone (United) Lighting Pty Ltd
600 Waverley Road
Chadstone
Melbourne

Christopher and Alexander's Lighting
Shop 146
Cnr. St Kilda & Alma Roads
St Kilda 3183
Victoria

Concord Lighting Pty Ltd
100 Harris
Pyrmont

Custom Lighting Pty Ltd
1167 High Street
Armadale
Victoria

Domalite Products
19 Daking St
North Parramatta
Sydney

Domus Lighting Pty Ltd
665 Forest Road
Bexley
Sydney

Edison Halo Lighting
30 Hansard
Waterloo
Sydney

Focus Lighting
28 Hansard Street
Waterloo
New South Wales

Fortune Lighting
30 Hansard Wtloo
New South Wales

For Lighting Pty Ltd
2-22 Balmain Street
Richmond
Victoria 3121

Guzzi Lighting
Novo Industries Pty Ltd
60 Bay Unit
Sydney

The House of Light
Unit 1
79-81 Frenchs Forest Road
Frenchs Forest
New South Wales 2086

King Georges Lighting
878 King Georges Road
South Hurstville
Sydney

Jolex Products Pty Ltd
553 Liverpool Road
South Stratfield
New South Wales 2136

Lamporama
274 Norton Street
Leichhardt
New South Wales

Lightcentre Pty Ltd
Box No. 108
Abbotsford
Victoria 3067

Low Voltage Lighting Co
5 Ridge Street
North Sydney

Lumiance
100 Harris Street
Pyrmont
Sydney

Lightmoves
Cnr Parramatte Road & Flood Street
Lchrdt
Sydney

Miranda Lighting
589 Kingsway
Miranda
Sydney

Lightworks Pty Ltd
12 McGowan Street
Melbourne

Lode Lighting
Lode & Co (Aust) Pty Ltd
89 Faraday St
Carlton
Melbourne

Mr Switches
604 Hawthorn Road
Brighton East
Melbourne

Murano
Italstyle Lighting Design
284 Victoria Street
Brunswick
Melbourne

Outdoor Lighting Centre Pty Ltd
123 Smith Street
Fitzroy
Victoria

R L M Lighting Pty Ltd
47 Alex Avenue
Moorabbin
Victoria 3067

Sun Lighting Industries
15 Garema Cct
Kingsbury
Sydney

Salon of Distinction
331 Camberwell Road
Camberwell
Melbourne

TC Metal Products (1984) Pty Ltd
3 Captain Cook Drive
Caringbah
New South Wales 2229

Zero Lighting
Style Finnish (Vic) Pty Ltd
485 Queensbery
North Melbourne

**NEW ZEALAND**
Arnold & Wright Ltd
PO Box 1081
Wellington

Custom Light Engineering Ltd
Private Bag 10057
Christchurch

Modus Lighting
PO Box 8374
Auckland

Authentic Designs
The Mill Road
West Rupert
VT 05776

B&P Lamp Supply, Inc.
McMinnville
TN 37110

Ball & Ball
463 W. Lincoln Highway
Exton
PA 19341

City Lights
2226 Massachusetts Avenue
Cambridge
MA 02140

Classic Lamp Posts
3645 N.W. 67th Street
Miami
FL 33147

Colonial Metalcrafters
Box 1135
Tyler
TX 75701

A.J.P. Coppersmith & Co
34 Broadway
Wakefield
MA 01880

Hurley Patentee Manor
R.D. 7, Box 98A
Kingston
NY 12401

King's Chandelier Company
Highway 14
PO Box 667
Eden (Leaksville)
NC 27288

Lamp Light
135 Yorkshire Court
Elyria
OH 44035

The London Venturers Company
2 Dock Square
Rockport
MA 01966

Gates Moore
River Road
Silvermine
Norwalk
CT 06850

Lighting Products
GTE Products Corporation
Sylvania Lighting Center
Danvers MA 01923

Paxton Hardware Ltd
7818 Bradshaw Road
Upper Falls
MD 21156

Progress Lighting
Box 12701
Philadelphia
PA 19134-1386

Rejuvenation House Parts
901 N. Skidmore
Portland
OR 97217

Renovation Concepts
213 Washington Avenue North
Minneapolis
MN 55401

Roy Electric Co., Inc.
1054 Coney Island Avenue
Brooklyn
NY 11230

The Saltbox
3004 Columbia Avenue
Lancaster
PA 17603

St Louis Antique Lighting Co.
801 N. Skinker
St Louis
MD 63130

Shaker Workshops
PO Box 1028
Concord
MA 01742

Stair & Co Ltd
940 Madison Avenue
New York
NY 10021

Sturbridge Yankee Workshop
Blueberry Road
Westbrook
ME 04092

Victorian Lighting Works
251 S. Pennsylvania Avenue
PO Box 469
Centre Hall
PA 16828

Virginia Metalcrafters
PO Box 1068
1010 E. Main Street
Waynesboro
VA 22980

Aladdin Lighting & Warehouse
Showroom
250 Speers
Toronto
Ontario

Au Courant
354 Davenport Road
Designers Walk
Toronto
Ontario

Artistic Glass
2112 Dundas W
Toronto
Ontario
M6R 1W9

Avenue Lighting
110 Avenue Road
Toronto
Ontario

BRE Lighting & Electrical
14840-115 Ave
Edmonton
Alberta

Celtic Art Glass
42 Forest Manor Road
Unit 12
Willowdale
Ontario
M2J 1M1

Centennial Lighting
2720 Millar Avenue
Saskatoon
S7K 4J4

Curtis Landscape Lighting
482 Parliament
Toronto
Ontario

Custom Lampshade Productions
5116 Dundas W
Toronto
Ontario

Electra-Art Lighting
1745 Keele
Toronto
Ontario

Gladu Electrical & Lighting Shop
2288 Lasalle Blvd
Sudbury
Ontario
P3A 2B1

Goosesales & Services Ltd
PO Box 370
Station B
Happy Valley
Labrador NFLD

Home Lighting Centre
306 University Avenue
Charlottetown, PEI
C1A 4MA

Lighting Unlimited
Yorkdale Shopping Centre
Atrium Place
Toronto
Ontario

Litemor
720, 17 Avenue SW
Calgary
Alberta

Living Lighting
1549 Avenue Road
Toronto
Ontario

Nimo's Lighting World
9737 Younge Street
Richmondhill
Ontario
L4C 1V7

Nippissing Lighthouse Ltd
131 McIntyre St E
North Bay
Ontario
P1B 1G5

The Old Lamp Shop
1582 Queen E
Toronto
Ontario

Raak Light
149 Church St
Toronto
Ontario

B A Robinson
2285 Cambe
Vancouver
V5Z 2T6

Sequence Lighting Ltd
28 Dunkirk Road
St Catherines
Ontario
L2R 1A1

Soo Lighthouse Ltd
102 Northern Avenue
Sault Ste, Marie
Ontario

Sunrise Lighting
910 Hanwell Road
Fredicton
New Brunswick
E3B 6A2

Sunrise Lighting
5755 Younge St
Halifax
Nova Scotia
B3K 1Z9

Superlite
1901 Logan Avenue
Winnipeg
Manitoba
R2R 0H6

Turn of the Century Lighting
112 Sherbourne
Toronto
Ontario

Ultra Lighting
1325 Eglinton Ave East
Mississauga
Ontario
L4W 4L9

Yorkdale Lighting
3350 Durrerin St
Toronto
Ontario

Ziggurat
254 King Street West
Toronto
Ontario

# GLOSSARY

**Accent light** Used for lighting specific objects, such as pictures or sculpture, or to highlight architectural features and other focal points within the room. Table lamps and directional ceiling-mounted lights can be used as accent lights. Accent lights are used in addition to general lighting.

**Amp** Short for amperes which measure electric current.

**Baffle** Shading on a light fitting to prevent glare. Often used on downlighters.

**Beam angle** Measurement of the spread of light from a bulb. The beam angle is twice the angle between the centre of the light beam and the point where the light level falls to half the power of the centre of the beam.

**Bulkhead fitting** A fitting mounted against a wall. Bulkhead fittings are usually covered by a protective metal grid and are designed for outdoor use.

**Compact fluorescent** A small fluorescent bulb, available in various shapes, for use in task lighting. Small fluorescents like this cannot be dimmed.

**Cross lighting** A method of lighting an object from two sources. The object for display is positioned where the beams from the two lights cross.

**Crown-silvered bulb** A conventional tungsten bulb, internally silvered around the widest part. This has the effect of beaming light back up against the fitting or shade, rather than down. Crown-silvered bulbs are useful for low pendants where the bulb might otherwise dazzle.

**Dichroic** A multi-mirror low-voltage bulb designed to pass the heat from the bulb upwards. Useful for rooms with low ceilings.

**Dimmer** A control for reducing the intensity of lighting. Not all types of lighting can be dimmed.

**Downlighter** A fitting fully or semi-recessed into the ceiling to direct light downwards. Available in a wide range of beam angles. The best form of general lighting.

**Drum** A small, drum-shaped uplighter designed for floor use. Good for shining light up through a display of plants.

**Eyeball** A small directional downlighter, semi-recessed so that it can be swivelled to direct light at an angle. Useful for accent lighting.

**Fluorescent** A glass tube coated with phosphor and containing an inert gas such as argon, krypton or neon plus mercury vapour at low pressure. When an electric current is passed through the light, the phosphor layer glows. Fluorescents are now available in daylight corrected versions, giving a kinder light than the original flat, harsh effect.

**Framing projector** A low-voltage fitting equipped with lenses and shutters, so that light can be directed in a very specific way. Shutters can be used to shape the light beam to the exact dimensions of the picture or object on display.

**GLS bulb** General lighting service bulb — the incandescent tungsten-filament light invented by Edison and still widely used today.

**Grolux** A fluorescent tube designed to encourage plants to grow when there is no other light.

**ISL bulb** Internally silvered reflector bulb, silvered from about half way up, so that all the light is directed downwards. Particularly suitable for spotlights intended for use as accents.

**Load** The total of all the wattages of all the bulbs used in a lighting circuit.

**Low-voltage** A bulb which runs on either 12 or 24 volts, much lower than the normal mains output of 240. These bulbs are small, so fittings are discreet, and are energy efficient. Because of the low voltage needed, a transformer must be used.

**Mercury vapour bulb** A bulb filled with mercury vapour, giving a greenish blue light. Used for special effects in garden lighting.

**Metal-halide bulb** A bulb made up of metal halides in a quartz tube. Gives a brilliant light, so often used for outdoor floodlighting.

**Multi-mirror bulb** A low-voltage bulb with integral reflectors.

**PAR bulb** PAR means parabolic aluminized reflector — a bulb with its own reflector to direct a strong beam of light. PAR bulbs are weatherproof, so particularly suitable for use in the garden.

**Reflector bulb** Any bulb with its own reflector. PAR, multi-mirror and ISL bulbs are all reflectors.

**Scoop reflector** A curved reflector, usually fitted to a wall washer, to make sure that light is spread to the top of the wall.

**Spotlight** Directional bulb, usually mounted on a track, or sometimes in a single fitting, allowing light to be beamed where it is needed.

**Task light** A fitting designed to cast light onto a work area.

**Track** A length of insulated electrical conductor which takes spotlights. Available in various sizes and designs.

**Transformer** A device for reducing mains power to low voltage.

**Tungsten bulb** The conventional GLS bulb.

**Tungsten strip light** A tungsten bulb in the shape of a strip, used for lighting beneath shelving and kitchen wall units.

**Tungsten-halogen bulb** A bulb with a tungsten filament filled with halogen gas. The gas combines with the tungsten to give a bright light. Sometimes called halogen quartz. These bulbs have a longer life than the conventional light bulb.

**Uplighter** A light fitting designed to beam light upwards, where it is reflected from the ceiling. Available in floor-standing, wall-mounted and tall versions.

**Volt** A unit used to measure the power of a circuit.

**Wall washer** A fitting designed to beam light evenly across a wall. Wall washers are usually ceiling-mounted. The wall itself acts as a reflector, shining light back into the room.

**Watt** A measurement used to describe the energy given by the appliance. In the case of light bulbs, it refers to the output of light.

## Acknowledgements

**Dunestyle Publishing Ltd** 13 right, 65 right, 82 left, 84, 86 **GTE Sylvania USA** 124, 129 **Kirsty McLaren** 18, 19 right, 20 left, 21 right, 43 bottom, 48, 72, 78, 79, 80 top, 81, 83, 85 **Oscar Woollens** Title page **Adrian Sankey** Contents page **Supplied by author** 53, 56, 57, 59, 61 right, 64, 65 left, 73 **Christopher Wray's Lighting Emporium**

The publishers have made every effort to ensure that all instructions given in this book are accurate and safe but they cannot accept liability for any resulting injury, damage or loss to either person or property whether direct or consequential and howsoever arising.

Dunestyle Publishing Ltd have endeavoured to observe the legal requirements with regard to the suppliers of photographic material.